SpringerBriefs in Computer Science

SpringerBriefs present concise summaries of cutting-edge research and practical applications across a wide spectrum of fields. Featuring compact volumes of 50 to 125 pages, the series covers a range of content from professional to academic. Typical topics might include:

- A timely report of state-of-the art analytical techniques
- A bridge between new research results, as published in journal articles, and a contextual literature review
- A snapshot of a hot or emerging topic
- An in-depth case study or clinical example
- A presentation of core concepts that students must understand in order to make independent contributions

Briefs allow authors to present their ideas and readers to absorb them with minimal time investment. Briefs will be published as part of Springer's eBook collection, with millions of users worldwide. In addition, Briefs will be available for individual print and electronic purchase. Briefs are characterized by fast, global electronic dissemination, standard publishing contracts, easy-to-use manuscript preparation and formatting guidelines, and expedited production schedules. We aim for publication 8–12 weeks after acceptance. Both solicited and unsolicited manuscripts are considered for publication in this series.

More information about this series at http://www.springer.com/series/10028

Arthur Francisco Lorenzon
Antonio Carlos Schneider Beck Filho

Parallel Computing Hits the Power Wall

Principles, Challenges, and a Survey of Solutions

 Springer

Arthur Francisco Lorenzon
Department of Computer Science
Federal University of Pampa (UNIPAMPA)
Alegrete, Rio Grande do Sul, Brazil

Antonio Carlos Schneider Beck Filho
Institute of Informatics, Campus do Vale
Federal University of Rio Grande
do Sul (UFRGS)
Porto Alegre, Rio Grande do Sul, Brazil

ISSN 2191-5768   ISSN 2191-5776   (electronic)
SpringerBriefs in Computer Science
ISBN 978-3-030-28718-4   ISBN 978-3-030-28719-1   (eBook)
https://doi.org/10.1007/978-3-030-28719-1

This Springer imprint is published by the registered company Springer Nature Switzerland AG.
The registered company address is: Gewerbestrasse 11, 6330 Cham, Switzerland

*This book is dedicated to the memory of
Márcia Cristina and Aurora Cera.*

Preface

Efficiently exploiting thread-level parallelism from modern multicore systems has been challenging for software developers. While blindly increasing the number of threads may lead to performance gains, it can also result in a disproportionate increase in energy consumption. In the same way, optimization techniques for reducing energy consumption, such as DVFS and power gating, can lead to huge performance loss if used incorrectly. In this book, we present and discuss several techniques that address these challenges. We start by providing a brief theoretical background on parallel computing in software and the sources of power consumption. Then, we show how different parallel programming interfaces and communication models may affect energy consumption in different ways. Next, we discuss tuning techniques to adapt the number of threads/operating frequency to achieve the best compromise between performance and energy. We finish this book with a detailed analysis of a representative example of an adaptive approach.

Alegrete, Brazil
Porto Alegre, Brazil

Arthur Francisco Lorenzon
Antonio Carlos Schneider Beck Filho

Acknowledgments

The authors would like to thank the friends and colleagues at Informatics Institute of the Federal University of Rio Grande do Sul and give a special thanks to all the people in the Embedded Systems Laboratory, who have contributed to this research since 2013.

The authors would also like to thank the Brazilian research support agencies, FAPERGS, CAPES, and CNPq.

Contents

Acronyms

CMOS	Complementary metal oxide semiconductor
DCT	Dynamic concurrency throttling
DSE	Design space exploration
DVFS	Dynamic voltage and frequency scaling
EDP	Energy-delay product
FFT	Fast fourier transform
FIFO	First-in first-out
FU	Function unit
GPP	General-purpose processors
HC	High communication
HPC	High-performance computing
ILP	Instruction-level parallelism
ISA	Instruction set architecture
LC	Low communication
MPI	Message passing interface
OpenMP	Open multi-programming
PAPI	Performance application programming interface
PPI	Parallel programming interface
PThreads	POSIX threads
RAM	Random access memory
SMT	Simultaneous multithreading
SoC	System-on-chip
TBB	Threading building blocks
TDP	Thermal design power
TLP	Thread-level parallelism

Chapter 1
Runtime Adaptability: The Key for Improving Parallel Applications

1.1 Introduction

With the increasing complexity of parallel applications, which require more computing power, energy consumption has become an important issue. The power
consumption of high-performance computing (HPC) systems is expected to significantly grow (up to 100 MW) in the next years [34]. Moreover, while general-purpose
processors are being pulled back by the limits of the thermal design power (TDP),
most of the embedded devices are mobile and heavily dependent on battery (e.g.,
smartphones and tablets). Therefore, the primary objective when designing and
executing parallel applications is not to merely improve performance but to do so
with minimal impact on energy consumption.

Performance improvements can be achieved by exploiting instruction-level
parallelism (ILP) or thread-level parallelism (TLP). In the former, independent
instructions of a single program are simultaneously executed, usually on a superscalar processor, as long as there are functional units available. However, typical
instruction streams have only a limited amount of parallelism [122], resulting in
considerable efforts to design a microarchitecture that will bring only marginal
performance gains with very significant area/power overhead. Even if one considers
a perfect processor, ILP exploitation will reach an upper bound [85].

Hence, to continue increasing performance and to provide better use of the extra
available transistors, modern designs have started to exploit TLP more aggressively
[7]. In this case, multiple processors simultaneously execute parts of the same
program, exchanging data at runtime through shared variables or message passing.
In the former, all threads share the same memory region, while in the latter each
process has its private memory, and the communication occurs by send/receive
primitives (even though they are also implemented using a shared memory context
when the data exchange is done intra-chip [21]). Regardless of the processor or
communication model, data exchange is usually done through memory regions that
are more distant from the processor (e.g., L3 cache and main memory) and have

A. Francisco Lorenzon, A. C. S. Beck Filho, *Parallel Computing Hits the Power Wall*,
SpringerBriefs in Computer Science, https://doi.org/10.1007/978-3-030-28719-1_1

higher delay and power consumption when compared to memories that are closer to it (e.g., register, L1, and L2 caches).

Therefore, even though execution time shall decrease because of TLP exploitation, energy will not necessarily follow the same trend, since many other variables are involved:

- Memories that are more distant from the processor will be more accessed for synchronization and data exchange, increasing energy related to dynamic power (which increases as there is more activity in the circuitry).
- A parallel application will usually execute more instructions than its sequential counterpart. Moreover, even considering an ideal scenario (where processors are put on standby with no power consumption), the sum of the execution times of all threads executing on all cores tends to be greater than if the application was sequentially executed on only one core. In consequence, the resulting energy from static power (directly proportional to how long each hardware component is turned on) consumed by the cores will also be more significant. There are few exceptions to this rule, such as non-deterministic algorithms, in which the execution of a parallel application may execute fewer instructions than its sequential counterpart.
- The memory system (which involves caches and main memory) will be turned on for a shorter time (the total execution time of the applications), which will decrease the energy resulting from the static power.

Given the aforementioned discussion, cores tend to consume more energy from both dynamic and static power, while memories will usually spend more dynamic power (and hence energy), but also tend to save static power, which is very significant [121]. On top of that, neither performance nor energy improvements resultant from TLP exploitation are linear, and sometimes they do not scale as the number of threads increases, which means that in many cases the maximum number of threads will not offer the best results.

On top of that, in order to speed up the development process of TLP exploitation and make it as transparent as possible to the software developer, different parallel programming interfaces are used (e.g., OpenMP—Open Multi-Processing [22], PThreads—POSIX Threads [17], or MPI—Message Passing Interface [38]). However, each one of these has different characteristics with respect to the management (i.e., creation and finalization of threads/processes), workload distribution, and synchronization.

In addition to the complex scenario of thread scalability, several optimization techniques for power and energy management can be used, such as dynamic voltage and frequency scaling (DVFS) [62] and power gating [47]. The former is a feature of the processor that allows the application to adapt the clock frequency and operating voltage of the processor on the fly. It enables software to change the processing performance to attain low-power consumption while meeting the performance requirements [62]. On the other hand, power gating consists of selectively powering down certain blocks in the chip while keeping other blocks powered up. In multicore processors, it switches off unused cores to reduce power consumption [84]. Therefore, in addition to selecting the ideal number of threads to execute an application, choosing the optimal processor frequency and turning off cores unused during the application execution may lead to significant reduction in energy consumption with minimal impact on performance.

1.2   Scalability Analysis

Many works have associated the fact that executing an application with the maximum possible number of available threads (the common choice for most software developers [63]) will not necessarily lead to the best possible performance. There are several reasons for this lack of scalability: instruction issue-width saturation; off-chip bus saturation; data-synchronization; and concurrent shared memory accesses [51, 64, 95, 114, 115]. In order to measure (through correlation) their real influence, we have executed four benchmarks from our set (and used them as examples in the next subsections) on a 12-core machine with SMT support. Each one of them has one limiting characteristic that stands out, as shown in Table 1.1. The benchmark hotspot (HS) saturates the issue-width; fast Fourier transform (FFT), the off-chip bus; MG, the shared memory accesses; and N-body (NB) saturates data-synchronization. To analyze each of the scalability issues, we considered the Pearson correlation [9]. It takes a range of values from $+1$ to -1: the stronger the "r" linear association between two variables, the closer the value will be to either $+1$ or -1. $r \geq 0.9$ or $r \leq -0.9$ means a very strong correlation (association is directly or inversely proportional). We discuss these bottlenecks next.

Issue-Width Saturation SMT allows many threads to run simultaneously on a core. It increases the probability of having more independent instructions to fill the function units (FUs). Although it may work well for applications with low ILP, it can lead to the opposite behavior if an individual thread presents enough ILP to issue instructions to all or most of the core's FUs. Then, SMT may lead to resource competition and functional unit contention, resulting in extra idle cycles. Figure 1.1a shows the performance speedup relative to the sequential version and the number of idle cycles (average, represented by the bars, and total) as we increase the number of threads for the HS application. As we start executing with 13 threads, two will be mapped to the same physical core, activating SMT. From this point on, as the number of threads grows, the average number of idle cycles increases by a small amount or stays constant. However, the total number of idle cycles significantly

Table 1.1 Pearson correlation between the scalability issues and each benchmark

	HS	FFT	MG	NB
Issue-width saturation	−0.92	−0.71	−0.79	−0.78
Off-chip bus saturation	−0.51	−0.98	−0.76	0.46
Shared memory accesses	−0.52	−0.43	−0.96	0.80
Data-synchronization	−0.54	−0.50	−0.59	0.97

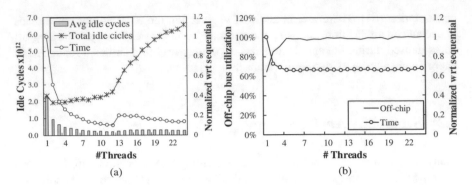

Fig. 1.1 Scalability behavior of parallel applications. (**a**) Issue-width saturation. (**b**) Off-chip bus saturation

increases. Because this application has high ILP, there are not enough resources to execute both threads concurrently as if each one was executed on a single core. They become the new critical path of that parallel region, as both threads will delay the execution of the entire parallel region (threads can only synchronize when all have reached the barrier). Therefore, performance drops and is almost recovered only with the maximum number of threads executing. In the end, extra resources are being used without improving performance and potentially increasing energy consumption, decreasing resource efficiency.

Off-Chip Bus Saturation Many parallel applications operate on huge amounts of data that are private to each thread and have to be constantly fetched from the main memory. In this scenario, the off-chip bus that connects memory and processor plays a decisive role in thread scalability: as each thread computes on different data blocks, the demand for off-chip bus increases linearly with the number of threads. However, the bus bandwidth is limited by the number of I/O pins, which does not increase according to the number of cores [41]. Therefore, when the off-chip bus saturates, no further improvements are achieved by increasing the number of threads [115]. Figure 1.2b shows the FFT execution as an example. As the number of threads increases, execution time and energy consumption reduce until the off-chip bus becomes completely saturated (100% of utilization). From this point on (4 threads), increasing the number of threads does not improve performance, as the bus cannot deliver all the requested data. There might be an increase in energy consumption as well since many hardware components will stay active while the cores are not being properly fed with data.

Shared Memory Accesses Threads communicate by accessing data that are located in shared memory regions, which are usually more distant from the processor (e.g., L3 cache and main memory), so they can also become a bottleneck. Figure 1.2 presents the number of accesses to the L3 cache (the only cache level shared among the cores) in the primary y-axis and the execution time normalized

Fig. 1.2 Scalability behavior of MG benchmark—shared memory accesses

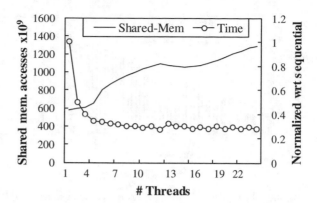

to the sequential execution in the secondary y-axis for the MG benchmark. When the application executes with more than four threads, the performance is highly influenced by the increased number of accesses to L3. Other factors may also influence L3 performance: thread scheduling, data affinity, or the intrinsic characteristics of the application. For instance, an application with a high rate of private accesses to L1 and L2 may also lead to an increase in the L3 accesses. Moreover, part of the communication may be hidden from the L3 when SMT is enabled: two threads that communicate and are executing on the same SMT core may not need to share data outside it.

Data-Synchronization Synchronization operations ensure data integrity during the execution of a parallel application. In this case, critical sections are implemented to guarantee that only one thread will execute a given region of code at once, and therefore data will correctly synchronize. In this way, all code inside a critical section must be executed sequentially. Therefore, when the number of threads increases, more threads must be serialized inside the critical sections. It also increases the synchronization time (Fig. 1.3a), potentially affecting the execution time and energy consumption of the whole application. Figure 1.3b shows this behavior for the n-body benchmark. While it executes with 4 threads or less, the performance gains within the parallel region reduce the execution time and energy consumption, even if the time spent in the critical region increases (Fig. 1.3a). However, from this point on, the time the threads spend synchronizing overcomes the speedup achieved in the parallel region.

1.2.1 Variables Involved

Considering the prior scenario, choosing the right number of threads to a given application will offer opportunities to improve performance and increase the energy efficiency. However, such task is extremely difficult: besides the huge number of

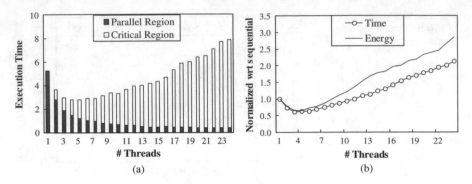

Fig. 1.3 Data-synchronization. (**a**) Critical section behavior. (**b**) Perf./Energy degradation

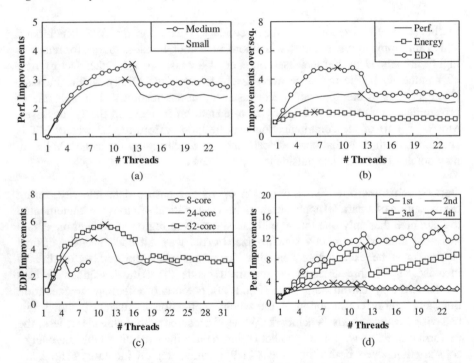

Fig. 1.4 Appropriate number of threads (*x*-axis) considering the improvements over sequential version (*y*-axis). (**a**) Different input sets. (**b**) Different metrics evaluated. (**c**) Different multicore processors. (**d**) Different parallel regions

variables involved, many of them will change according to different aspects of the system at hand and are only possible to be defined at runtime, such as:

- Input set: As shown in Fig. 1.4a, different levels of performance improvements for the LULESH benchmark [57] (also used as examples in the next two items) over its single-threaded version are reached with a different number of threads (*x*-

axis). However, these levels vary according to the input set (small or medium). While the best number of threads is 12 for the medium input set, the ideal number for the small set is 11.

- Metric evaluated: As Fig. 1.4b shows, the best performance is reached with 12 threads, while 6 threads bring the lowest energy consumption, and 9 presents the best trade-off between both metrics (represented by the energy-delay product (EDP)).
- Processor architecture: Fig. 1.4c shows that the best EDP improvements of the parallel application on a 32-core system are when it executes with 11 threads. However, the best choice for a 24-core system is 9 threads.
- Parallel regions: Many applications are divided into several parallel regions, in which each of these regions may have a distinct ideal number of threads, since their behavior may vary as the application executes. As an example, Fig. 1.4d shows the behavior of four parallel regions from the Poisson equation benchmark [94] when running on a 24-core system. One can note that each parallel region is better executed with a different number of threads.
- Application behavior: A DVFS enabled system adapts the operating frequency and voltage at runtime according to the application at hand, taking advantage of the processor idleness (usually provoked by I/O operations or by memory requests). Therefore, a memory- or CPU-bound application will influence the DVFS at different levels.

1.3 This Book

Efficiently exploiting thread-level parallelism from new multicore systems has been challenging for software developers. While blindly increasing the number of threads may lead to performance gains, it can also result in a disproportionate increase in energy consumption. In the same way, optimization techniques for reducing energy consumption, such as DVFS and power gating, can lead to huge performance loss if used incorrectly. For this reason, rightly choosing the number of threads, the operating processor frequency, and the number of active cores is essential to reach the best compromise between performance and energy. However, such task is extremely difficult: besides the large number of variables involved, many of them will change according to different aspects of the system at hand and are defined at runtime, such as the input set of the application, the metric evaluated, the processor microarchitecture, and the behavior of the parallel regions that comprise the application.

In this book, we present and discuss several techniques that address this challenge.

In Chap. 2, we provide a brief background for the reader. First, we give an overview of parallel computing in software, presenting the parallel programming interfaces widely used in multicore architectures. Second, we present the techniques used in software and hardware to optimize the power and energy consumption of parallel applications. Then, we describe the design space exploration of the optimization of parallel applications.

Chapter 3 assesses the influence of the parallel programming interfaces that exploit parallelism through shared variables (OpenMP and PThreads) or message passing (MPI-1 and MPI-2) on the behavior of parallel applications with different communication demands for embedded and general-purpose processors.

Chapter 4 presents the works that aim to optimize the execution of parallel applications by tuning the number of threads (DCT) or by selecting the ideal processor operating frequency through DVFS. We have conducted an extensive research considering studies published in the main conferences and journals over the past fifteen years. In this sense, more than fifty works were analyzed and classified into three classes according to the optimization method: only DCT, only DVFS, and the ones that apply both techniques.

Finally, in Chap. 5, we present in details, as a case study, Aurora, which is a new OpenMP framework that optimizes the performance, energy, or EDP of parallel applications by tuning the number of threads at runtime without any interference from the software developer.

Chapter 2
Fundamental Concepts

2.1 Parallel Computing in Software

Parallel programming can be defined as the process of dividing tasks of an application that can be executed concurrently, aiming to reduce their total execution time [97]. It has been widely used in the development of scientific applications that require large computing power, such as weather forecasting calculations, DNA sequences, and genome calculation. Moreover, with the popularization of multicore architectures, general-purpose applications (e.g., graphics editors and web servers) have also been parallelized.

The main goal of parallel computing is to use multiple processing units for solving problems in less time [36]. The key for parallel computing is the possibility to exploit concurrency of a given application by decomposing a problem into sub-problems that can be executed at the same time. As a simple example, suppose that part of an application involves computing the summation of a large set of values. In a sequential execution, all the values are added together in only one core, sequentially, as depicted in Fig. 2.1a. On the other hand, with the parallel computing, the data set can be partitioned, and the summations computed simultaneously, each on a different processor (C0, C1, C2, and C3, in Fig. 2.1b). Then, the partial sums are combined to get the final answer.

2.1.1 Communication Models

Parallel computing exploits the use of multiple processing units to execute parts of the same program simultaneously. Thus, there is cooperation between the processors that execute concurrently. However, for this cooperation to occur, processors should exchange information at runtime. In multicore processors, this can be done through shared variables or message passing [97]:

© The Author(s), under exclusive license to Springer Nature Switzerland AG 2019
A. Francisco Lorenzon, A. C. S. Beck Filho, *Parallel Computing Hits the Power Wall*,
SpringerBriefs in Computer Science, https://doi.org/10.1007/978-3-030-28719-1_2

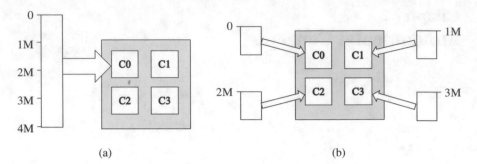

(a)   (b)

Fig. 2.1 Example of parallel computing. (**a**) Sequential execution. (**b**) Parallel execution in four cores

Shared variable is based on the existence of an address space in the memory that can be accessed by all processors. It is widely used when parallelism is exploited at the level of the thread since they share the same memory address space. In this model, the threads can have private variables (the thread has exclusive access) and shared variables (all the threads have access). When the threads need to exchange information between them, they use shared variables located in memory regions that are accessed by all threads (shared memory). Each parallel programming interface provides synchronization operations to control the access to shared variables, avoiding race conditions.

Message passing is used in environments where memory space is distributed or where processes do not share the same memory address space. Therefore, communication occurs using send/receive operations which can be point-to-point or collective ones. In the first, data exchange is done between pairs of processes. In the latter, more than two processes are communicating.

2.1.2 Parallel Programming Interfaces

The development of applications that can exploit the full potential parallelism of multiprocessor architectures depends on many specific aspects of their organization, including the size, structure, and hierarchy of the memory. Operating Systems provide transparency concerning the allocation and scheduling of different processes across the various cores. However, when it comes to TLP exploitation, which involves the division of the application into threads or processes, the responsibility is of the programmer. Therefore, PPIs make the extraction of the parallelism easier, fast, and less error-prone. Several parallel programming interfaces are used nowadays, in which the most common are Open Multi-Processing (OpenMP), POSIX Threads (PThreads), Message Passing Interface (MPI), Threading Building Blocks (TBB), Cilk Plus, Charm, among others.

OpenMP is a PPI for shared memory in C/C++ and FORTRAN that consists of a set of compiler directives, library functions, and environment variables [22]. Parallelism is exploited through the insertion of directives in the sequential code that inform the compiler how and which parts of the code should be executed in parallel. The synchronization can be implicit (implied barrier at the end of a parallel region) or explicit (synchronization constructs) to the programmer. By default, whenever there is a synchronization point, OpenMP threads enter in a hybrid state (Spin-lock and Sleep), i.e., they access the shared memory repeatedly until the number of spins of the busy-wait loop is achieved (Spin-lock), and then, they enter into a sleep state until the end of synchronization [22]. The amount of time that each thread waits actively before waiting passively without consuming CPU power may vary according to the waiting policy that gives the number of spins of the busy-wait loop (e.g., the standard value when *omp wait policy* is set to being active is 30 billion iterations) [86].

PThreads is a standard PPI for C/C++, where functions allow fine adjustment in the grain size of the workload. Thus, the creation/termination of the threads, the workload distribution, and the control of execution are defined by the programmer [17]. PThreads synchronization is done by blocking threads with mutexes, which are inserted in the code by the programmer. In this case, threads lose the processor and wait on standby until the end of the synchronization, when they are rescheduled for execution [117].

Cilk Plus is integrated with a C/C++ compiler and extends the language with the addition of keywords by the programmer indicating where parallelism is allowed. Cilk Plus enables programmers to concentrate on structuring programs to expose parallelism and exploit locality. Thus, the runtime system has the responsibility of scheduling the computation to run efficiently on a given platform. Besides, it takes care of details like load balancing, synchronization, and communication protocols. Unlike PThreads and OpenMP, Cilk Plus works at a finer grain, with a runtime system that is responsible for efficient execution and predictable performance [79].

TBB is a library that supports parallelism based on a tasking model and can be used with any C++ compiler. TBB requires the use of function objects to specify blocks of code to run in parallel, which relies on templates and generic programming. The synchronization between threads is done by mutual exclusion, in which the threads in this state perform busy-waiting until the end of synchronization [79].

MPI is a standard message passing library for C/C++ and FORTRAN. It implements an optimization mechanism to provide communication in shared memory environments [38]. MPI is like PThreads regarding the explicit exploitation of parallelism. Currently, it is divided into three norms. In *MPI-1*, all processes are created at the beginning of the execution and the number of processes does not change throughout program execution. In *MPI-2*, the creation of the processes occurs at runtime, and the number of processes can change during the execution. In *MPI-3*, the updates include the extension of collective operations to include nonblocking versions and extensions to the one-sided operations. Communication between MPI processes occurs through send/receive operations (point-to-point or collective ones), which are likewise explicitly handled by the programmers. When

MPI programs are executed on shared memory architectures, message transmissions can be done as shared memory accesses, in which messages are broken into fragments that are pushed and popped in first-in first-out (FIFO) queues of each MPI process [16, 21].

2.1.3 Multicore Architectures

Multicore architectures have multiple processing units (cores) and a memory system that enables communication between the cores. Each core is an independent logical processor with its resources, such as functional units, pipeline execution, registers, among others. The memory system consists of private memories, which are closer to the core and only accessible by a single core, and shared memories, which are more distant from the core and can be accessed by multiple cores [43]. Figure 2.2 shows an example of a multicore architecture with four cores (C0, C1, C2, and C3) and its private (L1 and L2 caches) and shared memories (L3 cache and main memory).

Multicore processors can exploit TLP. In this case, multiple processors simultaneously execute parts of the same program, exchanging data at runtime through shared variables or message passing. Regardless of the processor or communication model, data exchange is done through load/store instructions in shared memory regions. As Fig. 2.2 shows, these regions are more distant from the processor (e.g., L3 cache and main memory), and have a higher delay and power consumption when compared to memories that are closer to it (e.g., register, L1, and L2 caches) [61].

Among the challenges faced in the design of multicore architectures, one of the most important is related to the data access on parallel applications. When a private data is accessed, its location is migrated to the private cache of a core, since no other core will use the same variable. On the other hand, shared data may be replicated in multiple caches, since other processors can access it to communicate. Therefore, while sharing data improves concurrency between multiple processors, it also introduces the cache coherence problem: when a processor writes on any shared

Fig. 2.2 Basic structure of a multicore architecture with four cores

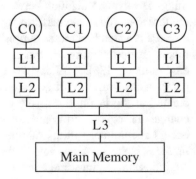

data, the information stored in other caches may become invalid. In order to solve this problem, cache coherence protocols are used.

Cache coherence protocols are classified into two classes: directory based and snooping [88]. In the former, a centralized directory maintains the state of each block in different caches. When an entry is modified, the directory is responsible for either updating or invalidating the other caches with that entry. In the snooping protocol, rather than keeping the state of sharing block in a single directory, each cache that has a copy of the data can track the sharing status of the block. Thus, all the cores observe memory operations and take proper action to update or invalidate the local cache content if needed.

Cache blocks are classified into states, in which the number of states depends on the protocol. For instance, directory based and snooping protocols are simple three-state protocols in which each block is classified into modified, shared, and invalid (they are often called as MSI—modified, shared, and invalid—protocol). When a cache block is in the modified state, it has been updated in the private cache, and cannot be in any other cache. The shared state indicates that the block in the private cache is potentially shared, and the cache block is invalid when a block contains no valid data. Based on the MSI protocol, extensions have been created by adding additional states. There are two common extensions: MESI, which adds the state "*exclusive*" to the MSI to indicate when a cache block is resident only in a single cache but is clean, and MOESI, which adds the "*state-owned*" to the MESI protocol to indicate that a particular cache owns the associated block and out-of-date in memory [43].

When developing parallel applications, the software developer does not need to know about all details of cache coherence. However, knowing how the data exchange occurs at the hardware level can help the programmer to make better decisions during the development of parallel applications.

2.2 Power and Energy Consumption

Two main components constitute the power used by a CMOS integrated circuit: dynamic and static [58]. The former is the power consumed while the inputs are active, with capacitances charging and discharging, which is directly proportional to the circuit switching activity, given by Eq. (2.1).

$$P_{\text{dynamic}} = CV^2 Af \qquad (2.1)$$

Capacitance (C) depends on the wire lengths of on-chip structures. The designers in several ways can influence this metric. For example, building two smaller cores on-chip, rather than one large, is likely to reduce average wire lengths, since most wires will interconnect units within a single core.

Supply voltage (*V* or *Vdd*) is the main voltage to power the integrated circuit. Because of its direct quadratic influence on dynamic power, supply voltage has a high importance on power-aware design.

Activity factor (*A*) refers to how often clock ticks lead to switching activity on average.

Clock frequency (*f*) has a fundamental impact on power dissipation because it indirectly influences supply voltage: the higher clock frequencies can require a higher supply voltage. Thus, the combined portion of supply voltage and clock frequency in the dynamic power equation has a cubic impact on total power dissipation.

While dynamic power dissipation represents the predominant factor in CMOS power consumption, static power has been increasingly prominent in recent technologies. The static power essentially consists of the power used when the transistor is not in the process of switching and is determined by Eq. (2.2), where the supply voltage is *V*, and the total current flowing through the device is I_{static}.

$$P_{static} = I_{static} x V \tag{2.2}$$

Energy, in joules, is the integral of total power consumed (*P*) over the time (*T*), given by Eq. (2.3).

$$Energy = \int_0^T P_i \tag{2.3}$$

Currently, energy is considered one of the most fundamental metrics due to the energy restrictions: while most of the embedded devices are mobile and heavily dependent on battery, general-purpose processors are being pulled back by the limits of thermal design power. Also, the reduction of energy consumption on HPC is one of the challenges to achieving the Exascale era, since the actual energy required to maintain these systems corresponds to the power from a nuclear plant of medium size [34]. Therefore, several techniques to reduce energy consumption have been proposed, such as DVFS and power gating.

2.2.1 Dynamic Voltage and Frequency Scaling

Dynamic voltage and frequency scaling is a feature of the processor that allows software to adapt the clock frequency and operating voltage of a processor on the fly without requiring a reset [62]. DVFS enables software to change system-on-chip (SoC) processing performance to attain low-power consumption while meeting the performance requirements. The main idea of the DVFS is dynamically scaling the supply voltage of the CPU for a given frequency so that it operates at a minimum speed required by the specific task executed [62]. Therefore, this can yield a significant reduction in power consumption because of the V^2 relationship shown in Eq. (2.2).

Reducing the operating frequency reduces the processor performance and the power consumption per second. Also, when reducing the voltage, the leakage current from the CPU's transistors decreases, making the processor most energy-efficient resulting in further gains [99]. However, determining the ideal frequency and voltage for a given point of execution is not a trivial task. To make the DVFS management as transparent as possible to the software developer, Operating Systems provide frameworks that allow each CPU core to have a min/max frequency, and a governor to control it. Governors are kernels models that can drive CPU core frequency/voltage operating points. Currently, the most common available governors are:

- *Performance*: The frequency of the processor is always fixed at the maximum, even if the processor is underutilized.
- *Powersave*: The frequency of the processor is always fixed at the minimum allowable frequency.
- *Userspace*: allows the user or any userspace program running to set the CPU for a specific frequency.
- *Ondemand*: The frequency of the processor is adjusted according to the workload behavior, within the range of allowed frequencies.
- *Conservative*: In the same way as the previous mode, the frequency of the processor is gradually adjusted based on the workload, but in a more conservative way.

Besides the pre-defined governors, it is possible to set the processor frequency level manually, by editing the configurations of the CPU frequency driver.

2.2.2 Power Gating

Power gating consists of selectively powering down certain blocks in the chip while keeping other blocks powered up. The goal of power gating is to minimize leakage current by temporarily switching power off to blocks that are not required in the current operating mode [59]. Power gating can be applied either at the unit-level, reducing the power consumption of unused core functional units or at the core-level, in which entire cores may be power gated [56, 76]. Currently, power gating is mainly used in multicore processors to switch off unused cores to reduce power consumption [84].

Power gating requires the presence of a header "sleep" transistor that can set the supply voltage of the circuit to ground level during idle times. Power gating also requires a control logic that decides when to power gate the circuit. Every time that the power gating is applied, an energy overhead cost occurs due to distributing the sleep signal to the header transistor before the circuit is turned off, and turning off the sleep signal and driving the voltage when the circuit is powered on again. Therefore, there is a break-even point, which represents the exact point in time where the cumulative leakage energy savings is equal to the energy overhead incurred by power gating. If, after the decision to power gate a unit, the unit stays idle for a time interval that is longer than the break-even point, then power gating saves energy. On the other hand, if the unit needs to be active again before the break-even point is reached, then power gating incurs an energy penalty [75].

Chapter 3
The Impact of Parallel Programming Interfaces on Energy

3.1 Methodology

3.1.1 Benchmarks

In order to study the characteristics of each PPI regarding the thread/process management and synchronization/communication, fourteen parallel benchmarks were implemented and parallelized in C language and classified into two classes: high and low communication (HC and LC). For that, we considered the amount of communication (i.e., data exchange), the synchronization operations needed to ensure data transfer correctness (mutex, barriers), and operations to create/finalize threads/processes.

Table 3.1 quantifies the communication rate for each benchmark (it also shows their input sizes), considering 2, 3, 4, and 8 threads/processes, obtained by using the Intel Pin Tool [74]. HC programs have several data dependencies that must be addressed at runtime to ensure correctness of the results. Consequently, they demand large amounts of communication among threads/processes, as it is shown in Fig. 3.1a. On the other hand, LC programs present little communication among threads/processes, because they are needed only to distribute the workload and to join the final result (as it is shown in Fig. 3.1b).

Since the way a parallel application is written may influence its behavior during execution, we have followed the guidelines indicated by [17, 36, 38] and [22]. The OpenMP implementations were parallelized using parallel loops, splitting the number of loops iterations (*for*) among threads. As discussed in [22], this approach is ideal for applications that compute on uni- and bi-dimensional structures, which is the case. Loop parallelism can be exploited by using different scheduling types that distribute the iterations to threads (static, guided, and dynamic) with different granularities (number of iterations assigned to each thread as the threads request them). As demonstrated in [69], the static scheduler with coarse granularity presents

A. Francisco Lorenzon, A. C. S. Beck Filho, *Parallel Computing Hits the Power Wall*, SpringerBriefs in Computer Science, https://doi.org/10.1007/978-3-030-28719-1_3

Table 3.1 Main characteristics of the benchmarks

Benchmarks		Operations to exchange data (Total per no. of threads/processes)				Input size
		2	3	4	8	
HC	Game of life	414	621	1079	1625	4096 × 4096
	Gauss–Seidel	20,004	20,006	20,008	20,016	2048 × 2048
	Gram–Schmidt	3,009,277	4,604,284	6,385,952	12,472,634	2048 × 2048
	Jacobi	4004	6006	8008	16,016	2048 × 2048
	Odd–even sort	300,004	450,006	600,008	1,200,016	150,000
	Turing ring	16,000	24,000	32,000	64,000	2048 × 2048
LC	Calc. of the PI number	4	6	8	16	4 billions
	DFT	4	6	8	16	32,368
	Dijkstra	4	6	8	16	2048 × 2048
	Dot-product	4	6	8	16	15 billions
	Harmonic series	8	12	16	32	100,000
	Integral-quadrature	4	6	8	16	1 billion
	Matrix multiplication	4	6	8	16	2048 × 2048
	Similarity of histograms	4	6	8	16	1920 × 1080

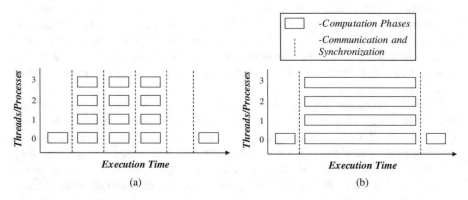

Fig. 3.1 Behavior of benchmarks. (**a**) High communication. (**b**) Low communication

the best results for the same benchmark set used in this study and, therefore, this scheduling mechanism is used here.

As indicated by [17, 36] and [38], we have used parallel tasks for the PThreads and MPI implementations. In such cases, the iterations of the loop were distributed based on the best workload balancing between threads/processes. Moreover, the communication between MPI processes was implemented by using nonblocking operations, to provide better performance, as showed in [44].

3.1.2   Multicore Architectures

3.1.2.1   General-Purpose Processors

Core2Quad   The Intel Core2Quad is an implementation of the $\times$86-64 ISA. In this study, the 45 nm Core2Quad Q8400 was used, which has 4 CPU cores running at 2.66 GHz, and a TDP of 95 W. It uses the Intel Core microarchitecture targeted mainly to desktop and server domains. It is a highly complex superscalar processor, which uses several techniques to improve ILP: memory disambiguation; speculative execution with advanced prefetchers; and a smart cache mechanism that provides flexible performance for both single and multithreaded applications.[1] As Fig. 3.2a shows, the memory system is organized as follows: each core has a private 32 kB instruction and 32 kB data L1 caches. There are two L2 caches of 2 MB (4 MB in total), each of them shared between clusters of two cores. The platform has 4 GB of main memory, which is the only memory region accessible by all the cores.

Xeon   The Intel Xeon is also an $\times$86-64 processor. The version used in this work is a 45 nm dual processor Xeon E5405. Each processor has 4 CPU cores (so there are 8 cores in total), running at 2.0 GHz, with a TDP of 80 W. It also uses the Core microarchitecture; however, unlike Core2Quad, Xeon processor E5 family is designed for industry-leading performance and maximum energy efficiency, since it is widely employed in HPC systems. The memory organization is similar to the Core2Quad (Fig. 3.2a): each core has a private 32 kB instruction and 32 kB data L1 caches. There are two L2 caches of 6 MB (12 MB in total), each of them shared between clusters of two cores. The platform has 8 GB of RAM, which is the only memory region accessible by all the cores.

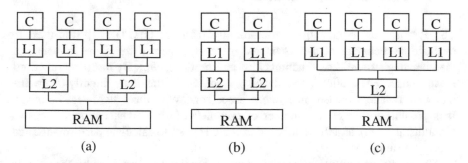

Fig. 3.2   Memory organization of each processor used in this study. (**a**) Intel Core2Quad and Xeon. (**b**) Intel Atom. (**c**) ARM Cortex-A9/A8

---

[1] Available at: http://www.intel.com/technology/architecture/coremicro.

3.1.2.2 Embedded Processors

Atom The Intel Atom is also an ×86-64 processor, but targeted to embedded systems. In this study, the 32 nm Atom N2600 was used, which has 2 CPU cores (4 threads by using Hyper-Threading support) running at 1.6 GHz, a TDP of 3.5 W. It uses the Saltwell microarchitecture, designed for portable devices with low-power consumption. Since the main characteristic of ×86 processors is the backward compatibility with the ×86 instructions set, programs already compiled for these processors will run without changes on Atom.[2] The memory system is organized as illustrated in Fig. 3.2b: each core has 32 kB instruction and 24 kB data L1 caches, and a private 512 kB L2 cache. The platform has 2 GB of RAM, which is the memory shared by all the cores.

ARM We consider the Cortex-A9 processor. ARM is the world's leading in the market of embedded processors. Designed around a dual-issue out-of-order superscalar, the Cortex-A family is optimized for low-power and high-performance applications.[3] The 40 nm ARM Cortex-A9 is a 32-bit processor, which implements the ARMv7 architecture with 4 CPU cores running at 1.2 GHz and TDP of 2.5 W. The memory system is organized as illustrated in Fig. 3.2c: each core has a private 32 kB instruction and 32 kB data L1 caches. The L2 cache of 1 MB is shared among all cores, and the platform has 1 GB of RAM. Since the ISA and microarchitecture of the Cortex-A8 and Cortex-A9 are similar, we also investigate the behavior of A8 based on the results obtained in the A9. The version considered is a 65 nm Cortex-A8 which has an operating frequency of 1 GHz, a TDP of 1.8 W.

3.1.3 Execution Environment

The Performance Application Programming Interface (PAPI) [14] was used to evaluate the behavior of processor and memory system without the influence of the operating system (i.e., function calls, interruptions, etc.). By inserting functions in the code, PAPI allows the developer to obtain the data directly from the hardware counters present in modern processors. With these hardware counters, it is possible to gather the number of completed instructions, memory accesses (data/instructions), and the number of executed cycles to calculate performance and energy consumption.

The energy consumption was calculated using the data provided by the authors in [13] (for the processors) and Cacti Tool (for the memory systems), as shown in Table 3.2. To estimate the total energy consumption (*Et*), we have taken into account

---

[2] Available at: http://www.intel.com/content/www/us/en/processors/atom/atom-processor.html.

[3] Available at: http://www.arm.com/products/processors/cortex-a/index.php.

Table 3.2 Energy consumption for each component on each processor

	ARM		Intel		
	Cortex-A8	Cortex-A9	Atom	Core2Quad	Xeon
Processor—static power	0.17 W	0.25 W	0.484 W	4.39 W	3.696 W
L1-D static power	0.0005 W	0.0005 W	0.00026 W	0.0027 W	0.0027 W
L1-I static power	0.0005 W	0.0005 W	0.00032 W	0.0027 W	0.0027 W
L2—static power	0.0258 W	0.0258 W	0.0096 W	0.0912 W	0.1758 W
RAM—static power	0.12 W	0.12 W	0.149 W	0.36 W	0.72 W
Energy per instruction	0.266 nJ	0.237 nJ	0.391 nJ	0.795 nJ	0.774 nJ
L1-D—energy/access	0.017 nJ	0.017 nJ	0.013 nJ	0.176 nJ	0.176 nJ
L1-I—energy/access	0.017 nJ	0.017 nJ	0.015 nJ	0.176 nJ	0.176 nJ
L2—energy/access	0.296 nJ	0.296 nJ	0.117 nJ	1.870 nJ	3.093 nJ
RAM—energy/access	2.77 nJ	2.77 nJ	3.94 nJ	15.6 nJ	24.6 nJ

the energy consumed for the executed instructions (E_{inst}), cache and main memory accesses (E_{mem}), and static energy (E_{static}), as given by Eq. (3.1).

$$Et = E_{inst} + E_{mem} + E_{static} \qquad (3.1)$$

To find the energy consumed by the instructions, Eq. (3.2) was used, where I_{exe} is the number of executed instructions multiplied by the average energy spent by each one of them ($E_{pcrinst}$).

$$E_{inst} = I_{exe} \times E_{perinst} \qquad (3.2)$$

The energy consumption for the memory system was obtained with Eq. (3.3), where ($L1DC_{acc} \times E_{L1DC}$) is the energy spent by accessing the L1 data cache memory; ($L1IC_{acc} \times E_{L1IC}$) is the same, but for the L1 instruction cache; ($L2_{acc} \times E_{L2}$) is for the L2 cache; and ($L2_{miss} \times E_{main}$) is the energy spent by the main memory accesses.

$$E_{mem} = (L1DC_{acc} \times E_{L1DC}) + (L1IC_{acc} \times E_{L1IC}) + (L2_{acc} \times E_{L2}) \qquad (3.3)$$
$$+ (L2_{miss} \times E_{main})$$

The static consumption of all components is given by Eq. (3.4). As static power is consumed while the circuit is powered, it must be considered during all execution time: (*#Cycles*) of application divided by the operating frequency (*Freq*). We have considered the static consumption of the processor (S_{CPU}), L1 data (S_{L1DC}) and instruction (S_{L1IC}) caches, L2 cache (S_{L2}), and main memory (S_{MAIN}).

$$E_{static} = \left(\frac{\#Cycles}{Freq}\right) \times (S_{CPU} + S_{L1DC} + S_{L1IC} + S_{L2} + S_{MAIN}) \qquad (3.4)$$

3.1.4 Setup

The results presented in the next section consider an average of ten executions, with a standard deviation of less than 1% for each benchmark. Their input sizes are described in Table 3.1. The programs were split into 2, 3, 4, and 8 threads/processes. Although most of the processors used in this work support only four threads, and are not commercially available in an 8-core configuration, it is possible to approximate the results by using the following approach: as an example, let us consider that we have two threads executing on one core only. These threads have synchronization points and when one thread gets there, it must wait for the other one and so on as long as there still are synchronization points. What it is done is to gather data of each thread executing on the core in between two synchronization points (which involves number of instructions, memory access, execution time, etc.). This behavior would be the same as if the two threads would be executing on two different cores, since the cores are homogeneous (i.e., have the same organization and, therefore, the same ILP exploitation capabilities). There may have context switches between both threads as they are executing, but they are not considered for the calculations (in the same way other services of the operating system are not considered).

Therefore, at the end of execution, we have all the data of each thread for each part of code in between synchronization points. We can calculate the energy consumption because we have the number of executed instructions, memory accesses, and so on, and we can infer the performance since we have the execution time of each part of code of each thread in between two synchronization points. For each part, we consider as execution time the one presented by the slowest thread (which simulates the behavior of one waiting for another if they were actually executing on two cores). This approach can be easily extrapolated to a larger number of threads.

The compiler used was the GCC-4.7.3 without optimization flags, to minimize the influence of the compiler on the PPIs. The following distributions were used: OpenMPI 1.6, OpenMP 3.0, and PThreads/POSIX.1-2008, running on the Linux Debian operating system.

It is important to highlight some observations regarding the results presented next:

- The benchmark set was developed and classified with the only purpose to evaluate each PPI regarding the thread/process management, workload distribution, and synchronization/communication.
- The versions of libraries, compilers, and tools used here have been updated since the experiments were performed.
- When this study was performed, we did not have access to processors that provide energy consumption directly from the hardware counters.

3.2 Results

3.2.1 Performance and Energy Consumption

Figures 3.3, 3.4, 3.5, 3.6, 3.7, 3.8, and 3.9 show the results of performance (in seconds) and energy (in Joules) of each processor and number of threads/processes ("1" means sequential execution) for the two benchmark classes (high and low communication). Figures 3.3 and 3.7 show raw numbers, where the x-axis of each chart is the energy consumption, and the y-axis is the execution time. Figures 3.4 and 3.8 demonstrate the fraction of energy consumed by each hardware component with respect to the total energy. Static and dynamic (S and D) energy for the processor and memory are considered. Also, Figs. 3.5 and 3.9 present the normalized performance and energy using the processor with the best results as the baseline. The results are discussed in detail in the next subsections, considering both classes of programs separately.

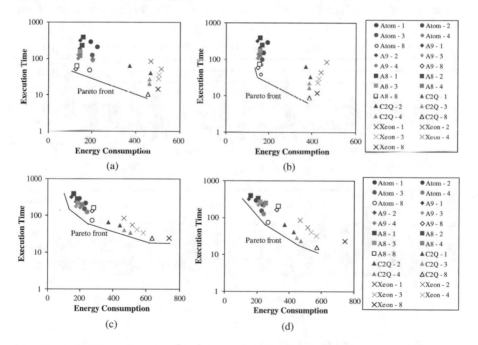

Fig. 3.3 Performance (seconds) and energy consumption (joules) results for high-communication programs. (**a**) OpenMP. (**b**) PThreads. (**c**) MPI-1. (**d**) MPI-2

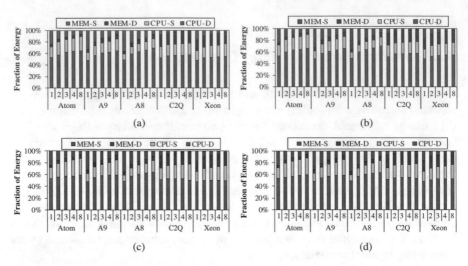

Fig. 3.4 Fraction of energy consumed by each hardware component (MEM: memory; CPU: processor; D: dynamic; S: static) for HC applications. (**a**) OpenMP. (**b**) PThreads. (**c**) MPI-1. (**d**) MPI-2

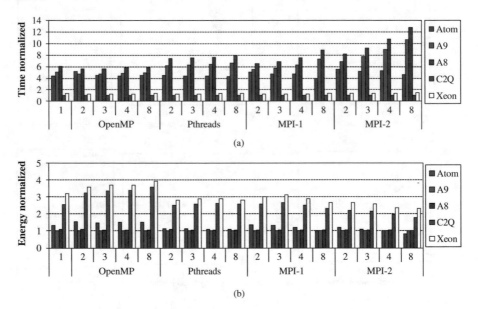

Fig. 3.5 Results normalized to Core2Quad (performance) and A9 (energy)—HC Programs. (**a**) Performance normalized to Core2Quad. (**b**) Energy consumption normalized to A9

3.2.1.1   High-Communication Programs

Figure 3.3 shows the performance and energy consumption for each processor running a different number of threads/processes. Each chart analyzes a different

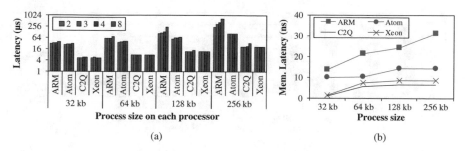

Fig. 3.6 Overhead to execute context switching on each processor. (**a**) Time to execute context switching. (**b**) Memory system latency for each process size during context switching

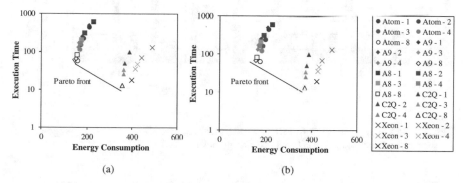

Fig. 3.7 Performance (seconds) and energy consumption (joules) results for low-communication programs. (**a**) Shared variables. (**b**) Message passing

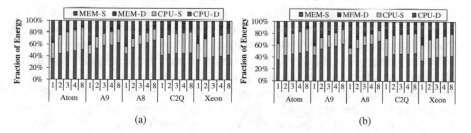

Fig. 3.8 Fraction of energy consumed by each component—LC applications (MEM: memory; CPU: processor; D: dynamic; S: static). (**a**) Shared variables. (**b**) Message passing

parallel programming interface. Considering the performance, regardless of the PPI used, all the processors performed better when exploiting a TLP of 8, and Core2Quad processor achieved the lowest execution time. Comparing the best case of each processor, Core2Quad is 4.32 times faster than Atom; 5.73 times faster than Cortex-A9; 6.87 times faster than Cortex-A8; and 1.34 times faster than Xeon. Considering only the embedded processors, Atom performed better, being 1.32 and 1.59 times faster than Cortex-A9 and A8, respectively.

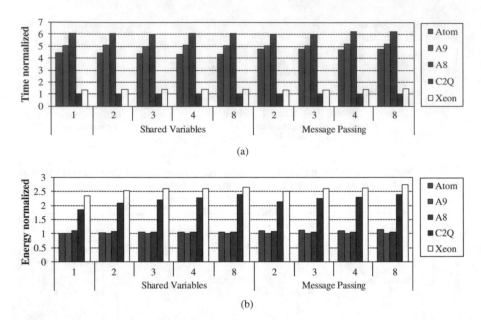

Fig. 3.9 Results normalized to Core2Quad (performance) and A9 (energy)—LC programs. (**a**) Performance normalized to Core2Quad. (**b**) Energy normalized to A9

When the energy consumption matters, embedded processors spend less energy than GPPs, and the A9 is the most efficient one. Considering the lowest energy consumption in each processor: A9 consumed 25% less energy than Atom; 8% less than A8; 61% less than Core2Quad; and 69% less energy than Xeon. In the most significant case, this difference is even greater: A9 consumed 55% less energy than Atom; 63% less than A8; 81% less than Core2Quad; and 84% less than Xeon. Moreover, the processors have different behaviors according to the PPI used: if the HC programs are parallelized using OpenMP, it is better to use the ARM Cortex-A9 exploiting a TLP of 8. In such case, the energy consumed is 35% lower than the best result in the Atom; and 5, 64, and 73% lower than the A8, Core2Quad, and Xeon, respectively. In another situation, when HC programs are parallelized using PThreads, MPI-1, or MPI-2, the lowest energy consumption is achieved by executing the sequential versions of the benchmarks on the Cortex-A9. Therefore, when it comes to energy and these interfaces, it is better to use one core even when there are more available.

In this application class, in which there are many accesses to the shared memory because of data exchange, the processor's performance and energy are highly influenced by the communication model (Fig. 3.3). For shared variables (OpenMP and PThreads), there are significant performance improvements, even though it does not increase in the same ratio as the TLP exploitation increases (i.e., when the number of threads is equal to 2, the execution time of a parallel version is greater than half of its sequential version and so on). In addition, parallel applications have similar energy consumption when one compares to their sequential counterparts in most cases. On the other hand, when using message passing (MPI-1 and MPI-2), even though there are performance gains, execution time decreases at a slower rate as the TLP increases, when compared to applications implemented using OpenMP and PThreads. The performance gains are limited by the excessive number of send/receive operations performed by communication, becoming a bottleneck. As a result of this poor performance improvements, energy consumption increases, compared to the sequential version, in all cases.

As there is no optimal combination of processor and number of threads/processes that offer at the same time the best performance with the lowest energy consumption, one must choose which metric is the most significant. In this way, the Pareto front is used in the charts. As Fig. 3.3 shows, it varies according to the PPI: in the OpenMP, there is only one combination offering the lowest energy consumption (Cortex-A9 executing 8 threads) and one with the best performance (Core2Quad, also running 8 threads). When other PPIs are used, the number of combinations is greater than three. Another interesting fact is that while we have few points when it comes to shared memory based PPIs (OpenMP and PThreads), the Pareto front is composed of several points when it comes MPI (Message Passing), increasing the complexity of finding the best trade-off in energy and performance.

Moreover, there are cases in which it is possible to reduce the energy consumption maintaining similar performance when embedded processors are chosen instead of GPPs. In the most significant case, it is possible to save 76% in energy by executing OpenMP HC programs on the Cortex-A9 with 8 threads instead of on the Xeon with 2 threads. On the other hand, if one chooses general-purpose instead of embedded processors aiming to reduce execution time, there is no single option available that will not result in huge increases in energy consumption. For instance, executing PThreads HC Applications with 8 threads on the Core2Quad instead of their OpenMP versions on the Cortex-A9 reduces execution time by 83%. However, it will increase the energy consumption by a factor of 3 times (304%).

In order to discuss how the processor and memory system influence each communication model and how they synchronize, let us first consider the programs that exchange data through shared variables. In OpenMP (Fig. 3.4a), threads come into a busy-waiting state, accessing the shared memory repeatedly until the end of synchronization [22]. This synchronization mechanism does not incur significant performance overhead, so all processors have similar behavior as TLP exploitation increases (as can be seen in Fig. 3.5a, the performance gap between the processors remains similar).

When it comes to energy, however, only in ARM processors the energy is reduced. For instance, while Cortex-A9 executing 8 threads saved almost 15% of energy and performed 6.15 times better than its sequential counterpart, on the Core2Quad, the energy increased 19% with similar performance improvements. This is because the energy consumed due to the extra executed instructions and accesses to the shared memory for the busy-waiting during synchronization have less influence in the ARM processors than in the Intel ones (Fig. 3.5a). While in the ARM processors these accesses were performed in the L2 cache, in the Intel processors they occurred in the main memory.

For PThreads (Fig. 3.3b), the context switching imposed by the mutex influenced more the performance in ARM processors than Intel ones. As more TLP is exploited, the performance gap between these two processors increases (Fig. 3.5a). In order to understand this behavior, LMbench (a suite to measure system performance) [80] was used to measure the impact of context switching on each processor. Figure 3.6a shows the latency of each context switching (logarithmic scale) considering processes with different parameters (which influences execution time, data size, etc.) and level of TLP exploitation. One can note that context switching (saving and restoring the contents of the register file, etc.) was slower on the ARM processors in all cases. This happens because the average latency to access the memory system is greater on the ARM than Intel processors, as shown in Fig. 3.6b. On the other hand, as PThreads access less the memory system during synchronization, the energy difference between all the processors remains almost the same as TLP exploitation increases (Fig. 3.5b). This means that for HC programs parallelized using PThreads, a more robust processor is the best choice, since it provides considerable performance improvements at the same price in the energy consumption. For instance, when TLP exploitation increases from 1 to 8, the performance difference between Core2Quad and Cortex-A9 increases 33% (4.88 to 6.52 times), while the energy gap remains the same.

In MPI-1 and MPI-2, the amount of send/receive operations performed by each processor to exchange data impacted in different ways the performance and energy consumption. Intel processors performed better than ARM ones, but spending more energy in most cases. As the number of processes increases, the performance gains are lower in ARM processors, increasing the performance difference between them and Intel ones (Fig. 3.5a), and influencing the energy consumption. In such cases, as more TLP is exploited, the energy difference between ARM and Intel decreases (Fig. 3.5b); and in the execution of 8 processes Atom got to a point where it consumed less energy than ARM processors. This scenario worsens when MPI-2 applications are executed (Fig. 3.3d), in which, as the number of processes increases, the performance gains are even lower in ARM processors. The reason for this is that dynamic process creation adds an overhead in the runtime in terms of executed instructions, mainly due to the communication using intercoms, which affects more ARM processors than Intel [19].

3.2.1.2 Low-Communication Programs

For LC programs, the performance and energy consumption for each communication model are very similar. In this way, results are separated only by communication model: shared variables and message passing (Fig. 3.7). As the applications are more CPU-bound, the impact of characteristics of each communication model on the memory system is reduced, highlighting the importance of the microarchitecture and operating frequency. In most cases, the overall performance increases in a similar ratio as more TLP is exploited (i.e., when the TLP exploitation is equal to 2, the execution time of parallel version is almost the half of sequential time and so on). However, when the number of threads/processes is 8, performance gains are impacted by the overhead of managing the parallelization (e.g., creation/termination of threads or processes), which is greater in message passing implementations, since the cost to manage processes is greater than threads [117].

All the processors perform better when they are running 8 threads/processes, and the Core2Quad continues offering the lowest execution time. Considering the best result of each processor, the performance difference between Intel processors is similar as observed for HC programs (Core2Quad is 1.37 times faster than Xeon; 4.32 times than Atom), while the performance gap between Intel and ARM diminishes in almost 13%. For instance, the difference between Core2Quad and Cortex-A9 decreases from 5.73 to 5.04 times, and from 6.87 to 6.04 times in relation to the Cortex-A8.

Unlike the HC programs, energy consumption decreases as TLP exploitation increases, regardless of the processor and communication model. In this way, all the processors consumed less energy when executing 8 threads/processes, and in the overall Cortex-A9 is the best choice. When one compares embedded and general-purpose processors, the energy difference between them increases as more TLP is exploited (Fig. 3.9b). When the number of threads increases, the memory system is more stressed and, therefore, spends more energy in Intel processors. As this class of applications has lower communication rate than the HC programs, it happens in a smaller proportion. Also, the performance difference between general-purpose and embedded processors decreases in almost 10% compared to the HC programs (e.g., 69 to 63% in the gap between A9 and Xeon).

In cases where the developer is looking for the best trade-off between energy and performance, there is no optimal choice. The same happens to HC programs (even though with more points and variations). As Fig. 3.7a shows, the Pareto front consists of three points in the results for shared variables. Two of them are the best choice for energy (Cortex-A9 with 8 threads) and performance (Core2Quad with 8 threads/processes). The other one (Atom running 8 threads) is the point that improves performance over the best choice in energy with minimal impact on it. On the other hand, if the designer aims to reduce the energy consumption maintaining similar execution time to the best possible, there is no satisfactory option available. For message passing (Fig. 3.7b), the Pareto front consists of only two points: one is the best energy possible (Cortex-A9), while the other is the lowest execution time (Core2Quad). This means that for this communication model, no option can improve a metric without causing a major impact on another. For instance, if the programmer wants to improve performance with minimal impact on energy, it will reduce the execution time by only 8%, increasing energy by a factor of 15%.

There are cases in which it is possible to use embedded instead of general-purpose processors to reduce the total energy consumption with little performance degradation. In the most significant case, energy can be reduced by 70% with minimal influence on performance, if a given LC program exploits a TLP of 4 or 8 executing on any embedded multicore rather than executing on the Core2Quad and Xeon with 1, 2, or 3 threads/processes, regardless of the communication model used.

3.2.2 Energy-Delay Product

As shown in the previous section, there is no optimal combination of processor and number of threads/processes that offer at the same time the best performance with the lowest energy consumption. Moreover, according to their niche, companies of general-purpose processors give more importance to performance, while the embedded ones to energy. In this case, the EDP may be useful since it correlates both metrics into a unique value. By adding an exponent x on delay (EDP = Energy $\times$ Delay^x), as the authors in [13] have already done (but considering only sequential applications), it is possible to change the weight of delay (performance) towards energy, which would reflect the importance given to performance considering the application field.

Figures 3.10, 3.11, 3.12, and 3.13 show the EDP for each processor as the importance of the delay is changed. The y-axis is the product of ED^x as the exponent (x) increases in the x-axis. Figure 3.10 shows the results of the sequential executions, while Figs. 3.11, 3.12, and 3.13 present the most representatives results for the parallel versions (2 and 8 threads/processes). Following the same methodology as before, HC programs are separated by PPI, while LC programs are separated by the geometric mean of the PPIs in each communication model. In overall, when both energy and performance are weighted equally (i.e., when $x = 1$), Core2Quad is the best choice (note that lower is better). Moreover, the difference between GPPs and embedded processors increases as the importance of performance towards energy increases (i.e., when the value of x increases). This reinforces the idea that GPPs

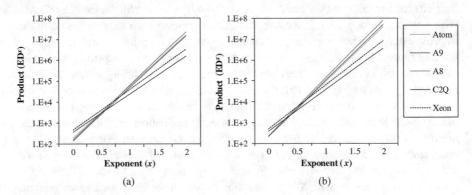

Fig. 3.10 Impact of exponent, x, on product ED^x—sequential execution. (**a**) High communication. (**b**) Low communication

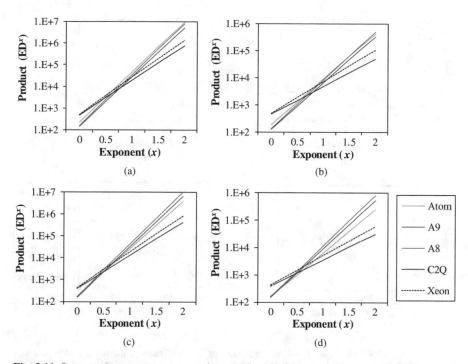

Fig. 3.11 Impact of exponent, x, on product ED^x of HC programs implemented with shared variables. (**a**) OpenMP—2 threads. (**b**) OpenMP—8 threads. (**c**) PThreads—2 threads. (**d**) PThreads—8 threads

are more focused on performance rather than energy, corroborating the authors' research in [13].

Let us discuss the results for the sequential versions (Fig. 3.10). For HC programs (Fig. 3.10a), Cortex-A9 provides the best ED^xP until $x = 0.6$. After that, Core2Quad outperforms all the processors. On the other hand, for LC programs (Fig. 3.10b), the Cortex-A9 provides the best ED^xP until $x = 0.1$, while Atom is better when x is greater than 0.1 and lower than 0.41. After that, Core2Quad outperforms all the processors. Therefore, the Core2Quad is the best choice even in a significant part where energy is more important than performance (0.41 < x < 0.99). Comparing only the embedded processors, in programs where memory system is more accessed (HC programs), the ARM A9 processor has better ED^xP than the Intel Atom for any value of x. On the other hand, when the applications use more the processor rather than memory (LC programs), Atom is the best choice in most cases.

As for the parallel versions (Figs. 3.11, 3.12, and 3.13), in all cases they achieved better ED^xP than their sequential counterparts, regardless of the number of threads/processes and communication model used. Let us first consider the results when the processors are executing HC programs using shared variables. In OpenMP implementations (Fig. 3.11a and b), Cortex-A9 has better ED^xP than the other

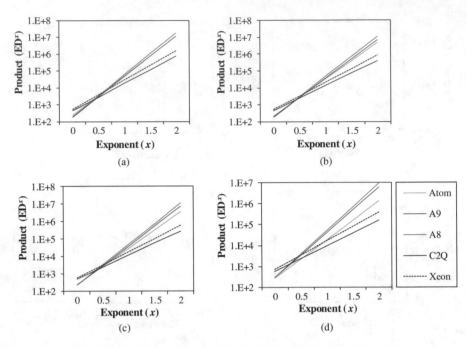

Fig. 3.12 Impact of exponent, x, on product ED^x of HC programs implemented with message passing. (**a**) MPI-1—2 processes. (**b**) MPI-1—8 processes. (**c**) MPI-2—2 processes. (**d**) MPI-2—8 processes

embedded processors, no matter the value of x. In addition, as the number of threads increases, the more important must be the performance (i.e., higher values for x) so the GPPs can present better EDP than the embedded ones (see Table 3.3). For PThreads implementations, the behavior is different (Fig. 3.11c and d): Cortex-A9 has the best EDP only when $x < 0.36$ and $x < 0.19$ for 2 and 8 threads, respectively. After that, Atom is better until $x = 0.55$ and $x = 0.61$, for 2 and 8 threads, respectively. When x is greater than these values, Core2Quad outperforms all the processors.

Figure 3.12 shows the results when HC programs are implemented with message passing. Let us first discuss the MPI-1 results, where the GPPs outperform embedded ones at a very similar value of x as the one presented in PThreads. Considering embedded processors only, the one that offers the best $ED^x P$ changes as the number of threads increase, regardless the importance of x. In the execution of 2 processes, Cortex-A9 has the best $ED^x P$, while with 8 processes, Atom is the best choice. The reason for that has already been discussed in Sect. 3.2.1: as more TLP is exploited, the performance loss and the increases in the energy consumption are more significant in ARM processors than in the Intel ones.

When it comes to the LC programs (Fig. 3.13), Core2Quad continues offering the best $ED^x P$ in most cases (mainly when performance and energy have the

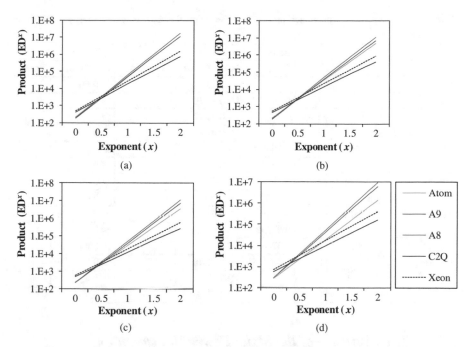

Fig. 3.13 Impact of exponent, x, on product ED^x of LC programs. (**a**) Shared variables—2 threads. (**b**) Shared variables—8 threads. (**c**) Message passing—2 processes. (**d**) Message passing—8 processes

same weight). Comparing only the embedded processors: when they communicate through shared variables, Atom processor has better ED^xP than ARM when $x > 0.38$ and $x > 0.47$ for 2 and 8 threads, respectively. On the other hand, for the results using message passing, Cortex-A9 has the best ED^xP in the execution with 2 processes regardless of the performance importance. When TLP exploitation increases to 8, Atom once again outperforms Cortex-A9 for $x > 1.35$. Therefore, there are specific scenarios where the best choice is one processor or another. When the general-purpose processors are compared, Core2Quad has better ED^xP than Xeon in all cases.

Table 3.3 shows the intersection points to figure out which is the best processor in between the intervals of x considering the charts of Figs. 3.10, 3.11, 3.12, and 3.13. In overall, when performance is the most important parameter ($x > 1$), it is true that GPP is always the best choice. However, as already discussed, looking at the other side (energy), it depends on how much energy matters for the designer.

Table 3.3 Intervals of x where each processor is better on the $ED^x P$, when energy is the most important

		TLP	Embedded processors			GPPs	
			Atom	Cortex-A9	Cortex-A8	Core2Quad	Xeon
HC		1	–	0.0–0.60	–	> 0.60	–
LC		1	0.10–0.41	0.0–0.10	–	> 0.41	–
HC	OMP	2	–	0.0–0.77	–	> 0.7	–
Shared variables		8	–	0.0–0.81	–	> 0.81	–
Figure	PT	2	0.36–0.55	0.0–0.36	–	> 0.55	–
		8	0.19–0.61	0.0–0.19	–	> 0.61	–
HC	MPI-1	2	–	0.0–0.56	–	> 0.56	–
Message passing		8	0.0–0.61	–	–	> 0.61	–
Figure	MPI-2	2	–	0.0–0.42	–	> 0.42	–
		8	0.0–0.49	–	–	> 0.49	–
LC	SV	2	0.37–0.48	–	–	> 0.49	–
Figure		8	0.48–0.56	0.0–0.48	–	> 0.56	–
	MP	2	–	0.0–0.42	–	> 0.42	–
		8	–	0.0–0.49	–	> 0.49	–

3.2.3   The Influence of the Static Power Consumption

In this section, we present a study regarding the influence of the static power on the total energy consumption of different multicore processors. First, we briefly discuss what static power is and how it can affect the energy consumption of parallel applications. Next, the methodology used in this experiment is presented, followed by a discussion about the results achieved.

As already discussed in Sect. 2.2, there are two main components that constitute the power used by a CMOS integrated circuit: dynamic and static. The former is the power consumed while the inputs are active, with capacitance charging and discharging, being directly proportional to the circuit switching activity. The static power derives from the length of the transistor channel as well as the doping level and gate thickness. As an example, although increasing doping level allows higher on current for faster transitions, it also causes more considerable leakage. Therefore, companies can tune the circuits during the manufacturing process to be faster and consume more static power or vice versa [83]. In some cases, the static power in the processor may represent up to 40% of the total energy consumption [35, 60, 83].

TLP exploitation in multicore systems affects dynamic and static power consumption in different ways. The former will most likely increase as the number of threads increase, since additional memory accesses and executed instructions are necessary for synchronization and data exchange. On the other hand, memory will consume less static power because it will be powered for a shorter period because of overall performance improvements. However, since parallelization is not perfect, some threads distributed over the processors will take longer to execute than others.

Table 3.4 Respective energy consumed per instruction and static power when changing the importance of static power of processor

		10%	20%	30%	40%
Atom	Static power (W)	0.242	0.484	0.726	0.968
	Energy per instruction (nJ)	0.448	0.391	0.335	0.276
Cortex-A9	Static power (W)	0.125	0.250	0.375	0.500
	Energy per instruction (nJ)	0.291	0.237	0.183	0.129
Cortex-A8	Static power (W)	0.085	0.170	0.255	0.340
	Energy per instruction (nJ)	0.338	0.266	0.195	0.124
Core2Quad	Static power (W)	2.195	4.390	6.585	8.780
	Energy per instruction (nJ)	1.267	1.126	0.985	0.845
Xeon	Static power (W)	1.848	3.696	5.544	7.392
	Energy per instruction (nJ)	1.419	1.261	1.103	0.946

In such cases, the sum of all amounts of static power consumed by all the processors will be larger than its sequential counterpart.

Considering the aforementioned scenario, this section aims to investigate the influence of the static power consumption of the processor on parallel applications in multicore systems. We consider four different proportions of static power in respect to the total power consumption of the processor obtained from [13] and CACTI 5.1[4]: 10, 20, 30, and 40%. Table 3.4 shows the static power and the energy consumption per instruction when different ratios of static/dynamic power are considered. When the proportion of static power increases in respect to the total power consumption of the processor, dynamic (energy per executed instruction) will decrease in the same amount; therefore, total energy consumption will always be the same. This analysis involves power in the core only: the ratio of static/dynamic power consumption of the memory system is not changed.

The results consider the geometric mean of each communication model, since the behavior is very similar between the interfaces that implement them (standard deviation lower than 1%). Figures 3.14 and 3.15 show the impact of static power for each communication model on each processor in HC and LC programs, respectively. All the charts consider the results when the static power of the processor is fixed to 10% as baseline, and show the impact on the total energy consumption when it is changed to 20, 30, and 40%. Therefore, values lower than "1" mean that there are energy savings.

In overall, the architecture of the processors influences how the static power impacts the total energy consumption. In Intel processors, increasing the importance of static power will also increase energy consumption, while one can observe the opposite behavior for ARM processors. The amount of TLP also changes the variation ratio: the more TLP is exploited, the more significant the impact when changing the amount of static power on the total energy consumption. As the

---

[4]Available at: http://www.hpl.hp.com/techreports/2008/HPL-2008-20.html.

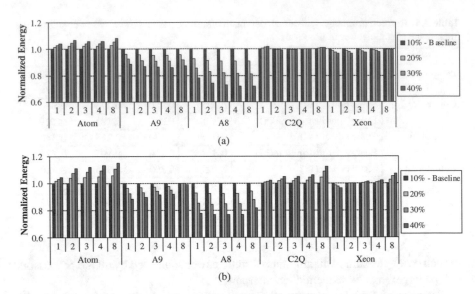

Fig. 3.14 Impact on the total energy consumption when the static power of processor varies from 10%—HC Programs. (**a**) Shared variables. (**b**) Message passing

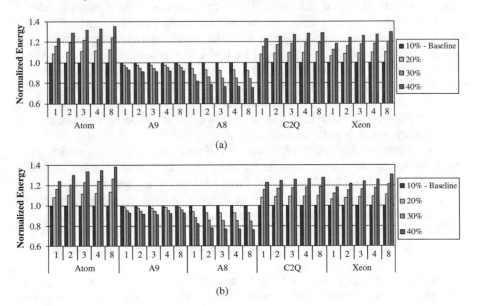

Fig. 3.15 Impact on the total energy consumption when the static power of processor varies from 10%—LC programs. (**a**) Shared variables. (**b**) Message passing

parallelization is not perfect, the sum of the static power consumed by all cores is larger than if it was sequentially executed. It means that the static power consumed by the processors starts to be more important as more TLP is exploited.

Table 3.5 Number of executed instructions by core per second

Comm. model	TLP	HPC programs					LC programs				
		Atom	A9	A8	C2Q	Xeon	Atom	A9	A8	C2Q	Xeon
Shared variables	2	837	899	749	4018	3286	432	744	620	1916	1441
	3	875	893	743	3969	3197	427	747	623	1880	1428
	4	887	882	735	3924	3136	432	718	598	1849	1421
	8	835	840	700	3770	2973	431	717	598	1838	1394
Message passing	2	720	807	672	3376	2945	410	745	621	1955	1525
	3	696	754	628	3347	2842	405	738	615	1932	1502
	4	671	729	607	3262	2780	407	708	590	1911	1462
	8	640	599	499	2759	2440	404	702	584	1892	1365
Sequential		884	905	754	3625	3342	419	733	611	1936	1541

Table 3.6 The proportion of the number of executed instructions by core per second in the parallel versions regarding its sequential version

Comm. model	TLP	HPC programs					LC programs				
		Atom	A9	A8	C2Q	Xeon	Atom	A9	A8	C2Q	Xeon
Shared variables	2	0.95	0.99	0.99	1.11	0.98	1.03	1.02	1.01	0.99	0.94
	3	0.99	0.99	0.99	1.09	0.96	1.02	1.02	1.02	0.97	0.93
	4	1.00	0.97	0.97	1.08	0.94	1.03	0.98	0.98	0.96	0.92
	8	0.94	0.93	0.93	1.04	0.89	1.03	0.98	0.98	0.95	0.90
	AVG	0.97	0.97	0.97	1.08	0.94	1.03	1.00	1.00	0.97	0.92
Message passing	2	0.81	0.89	0.89	0.93	0.88	0.98	1.02	1.02	1.01	0.99
	3	0.79	0.83	0.83	0.92	0.85	0.97	1.01	1.01	1.00	0.97
	4	0.76	0.80	0.80	0.90	0.83	0.97	0.97	0.97	0.99	0.95
	8	0.72	0.66	0.66	0.76	0.73	0.96	0.96	0.96	0.98	0.89
	AVG	0.77	0.79	0.79	0.88	0.82	0.97	0.99	0.99	0.99	0.95
Sequential		1	1	1	1	1	1	1	1	1	1

Let us first discuss the results of the Intel processors executing HC programs (Fig. 3.14). In such cases, the effect of changing the proportion of static power is negligible in most cases. To better understand that, let us consider Tables 3.5 and 3.6. The former presents the number of executed instructions by core per second. To compare only the behavior of each PPI on each processor, Table 3.6 depicts the number of instructions executed per second in the parallel version by its sequential counterpart, the bigger the result, the closer it is to the behavior of its sequential version, meaning that the processor will be executing more instructions instead of waiting for sync and data exchange.

When doing this calculation, we can note that the LC programs have bigger values than HC programs—which means that, even though they execute less instructions per second (Table 3.5) because of the kind of application, their parallel versions proportionally execute more instructions per second than the HC applications, which shows that they spend less time waiting for data exchange or sync. This can be observed for the message passing in Tables 3.5 and 3.6: the higher the amount of executed processes, the higher the load imbalance, and the smaller is the number of executed instructions per second. In this case, static power plays an important role. When it comes to the ARM processors executing HC programs (Fig. 3.14), the results show that in all cases, increasing static power of the processor reduces the total energy consumption. The reason for this is that the reduction in the dynamic power consumption is greater than the increase provided by the change in the value of the static power in the processor.

For the LC programs (Fig. 3.15), the impact of changing the amount of static power is greater than the observed for the HC programs. In addition, the same behavior is observed regardless of the communication model used. Considering the Intel processors, the higher the TLP exploitation, the greater the impact of increasing the static power of the processor. In the sequential version, when the static power changes from 10 to 40%, the total energy consumption increases by almost 24% on both Atom and Core2Quad, and 18% in the Xeon processor. As for the execution with eight threads/processes, this energy difference is even higher: 35 and 38% for shared variables and message passing, respectively, in the Atom processor; and 28 and 30% in the Core2Quad and Xeon, respectively, regardless of the communication model. As for ARM processors, which have a high number of executed instructions per second (see Table 3.5), changing the static power of the processor from 10 to 40% results in energy savings in all cases: almost 8% in the Cortex-A9 and 24% in the Cortex-A8.

Analyzing the whole scenario, Intel and ARM processors have different behaviors when the proportion of static power is changed in respect to the total power consumption. In the former, regardless of the kind of application and the communication model used, keeping static power of the processor as low as possible saves energy in most cases, even though at different levels. On the other hand, for ARM processors, the higher the static power, the greater the reduction in energy consumption.

3.3 Discussion

This chapter performed a static exploration for optimal combinations of processors, communication models, and TLP exploitation to reach the best results in performance, energy, and EDP. A great number of variables were considered: 5 multicore processors with different microarchitectures and ISAs; 14 parallel benchmarks classified according to the communication rate; four parallel programming interfaces classified into two classes of communication models; different levels of TLP exploitation; and four different levels of static power of the processor. We demonstrated that even though there are combinations with the best performance and the lowest energy consumption, there is no single one that offers the best result for both at the same time. However, we found some significant results, summarized next.

Let us first discuss performance and energy (Sect. 3.2.1), in which the most robust processor (Core2Quad) achieved the lowest execution time, while the embedded processor Cortex-A9 consumed less energy in all cases. For HC applications, the PPIs matter: PThreads has shown to be the best choice for all Intel processors (GPP or embedded), since it provides considerable performance improvements over the others at the same price of energy consumption as the sequential version. On the other hand, when exploiting parallel loops, OpenMP is better for ARM processors, since the impact of the busy-waiting mechanism is lower on these processors than on the Intel ones. In overall, MPI is the worst choice for all the processors, presenting poor scalability: as TLP exploitation increases, performance gains are limited by its message based communication, and energy consumption increases when compared to its sequential version. It was expected that MPI would perform worse than OpenMP and PThreads in HC applications on shared memory environments. This behavior happens because each communication between MPI processes involves an additional cost related to the construction/deconstruction of the message as well as the message transmission.

There are different situations when analyzing the Pareto front for all the cases. In OpenMP applications, it contains only two points: the best result for performance (Core2Quad running 8 threads) and the best for energy consumption (Cortex-A9, also executing 8 threads). There is no option that it will not influence considerably a metric to improve another. For the other PPIs, there are more points to be explored, and the impact on a metric to improve another is minimal. For instance, in MPI-1 applications with 8 processes, it is possible to reduce the energy consumption in 15% without impact on performance by changing processors (Core2Quad instead of Xeon).

The scenario is different for LC benchmarks. For those, what matters is the communication model rather than a specific PPI. Since they are more CPU-bound, how the processor can exploit ILP and its operating frequency gain in importance. Regardless of the PPI, performance increases and energy reduces as the TLP increases, resulting in better EDP. Therefore, even though these applications scale better than HC ones, the design space is more restricted, offering less opportunities for optimization. The Pareto front has fewer points and alternatives to optimize a metric with minimal impact on another, and the differences between Intel and ARM processors are subtler.

When it comes to $ED^x P$ (energy-delay^x product, depicted in Sect. 3.2.2), in all cases (no matter the processor or PPI used) the parallel versions were better than their sequential counterparts, if one considers that performance has the same weight as energy ($x = 1$), and the difference in EDP between a parallel version and its sequential counterpart increases as more importance is given to performance. The Core2Quad processor has better $ED^x P$ in this case, regardless of the communication model used or the number of threads/processes.

In general, GPPs are always the best choice when targeting performance only. However, looking at the other side (energy), it depends on how much energy matters to the designer. For instance, in HC programs using PThreads, three processors have the best $ED^x P$ according to the importance of energy: Cortex-A9 for $x < 0.36$;

Atom for $0.36 < x < 0.55$; Core2Quad for larger values of x. In some scenarios, Core2Quad is the best choice even if energy is more important ($x < 1$). However, as the number of threads increase, more importance to performance must be given (the x value must get closer to 1) so the Core2Quad still presents the best $ED^x P$.

The PPIs influence EDP in different aspects. For OpenMP, energy consumption in the memory system is very important, because of the busy-waiting. For PThreads, on the other hand, a more robust processor will decrease context switching time. For the MPI versions of the applications, as more threads execute, EDP in general worsens for ARM processors and improves for Intel ones, since the impact of the communication on the former is more evident.

In Sect. 3.2.3, we demonstrated that processors present different behaviors when tuning the values of energy resultant from the static and dynamic power of the processor. For Intel processors, by keeping the static power of the processor as low as possible, more energy will be saved. In the most significant case, it is possible to save 38% of energy if the hardware designer keeps the static power at 10% instead of 40%. On the other hand, the opposite happens for the ARM processors, where the higher the static power, the lower the total energy. For instance, it is possible to save 28% of energy if the static power represents 40% of the total energy, instead of 10%. The number of executed threads also influences results: as more TLP is exploited, more impact it has on tuning the static power. These results are directly related to how long the processor spends time synchronizing and communicating. Therefore, HC applications are more susceptible to changes in static power.

Chapter 4
Tuning Parallel Applications

4.1 Design Space Exploration of Optimization Techniques

Design space exploration (DSE) generally consists of a multi-objective optimization problem, composed of several parameters that must be tuned to present the best trade-off regarding the selected metrics, such as energy, performance, and EDP[87]. Figure 4.1 shows a schematic illustration of the DSE process. Firstly, the input data that should be evaluated are provided to the DSE. These values are calculated through any classification model, such as neural network, linear regression, and mathematical models. Then, the DSE outputs results containing the best trade-offs between the values and metrics.

The DSE phase can be performed in different moments of the application execution. It can use offline or online information provided by the processor architecture and the execution of an application, and with or without adaptation at runtime. Furthermore, it can also be transparent or not: transparency is related to the need for special tools or compilers, programmer influence, or change in the source or binary codes in any of the DSE phases. In this book, we classify the strategies used to optimize parallel applications into two groups, as described below.

No Runtime Adaptation and no Transparency In this kind of approach, the DSE is fully performed before the application execution. It comprises prediction models which use a variety of statistical models to analyze current and historical values of the target architecture and applications to make predictions. However, the data obtained by the prediction are used only to decide the best configuration to run an application. Therefore, there is no decision-making and adaptation of the parallel application at runtime. A predictive model consists of four necessary steps, as Fig. 4.2 shows. In the first step, data from the architecture and applications are collected to generate the model. Then, a statistical model is formulated by applying some method (e.g., linear regression or a neural network) over the collected data. After, predictions are made for the new input data. In the last step, additional data

© The Author(s), under exclusive license to Springer Nature Switzerland AG 2019   41
A. Francisco Lorenzon, A. C. S. Beck Filho, *Parallel Computing Hits the Power Wall*,
SpringerBriefs in Computer Science, https://doi.org/10.1007/978-3-030-28719-1_4

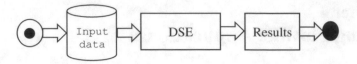

Fig. 4.1 Design space exploration process

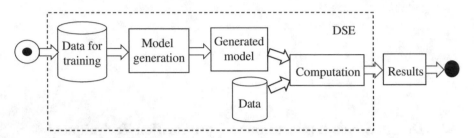

Fig. 4.2 No runtime adaptation and no transparency

are used to validate the model. Because such approaches rely on the need for special compilers, tools, or programmer influence, they do not present transparency to the user.

Runtime Adaptation and/or Transparency In this class of approaches, the models consider information from the behavior (e.g., architecture, OS, and application) obtained before the application execution or at runtime to make decisions and adjust the application execution. In this case, different characteristics of the application that are only known at runtime, such as the length of the input, can be considered. Adaptation using dynamic information is essential for applications with variable behavior, in which the workload constantly changes, and with many parallel regions, in which each of them may have different behavior. Such adaptation processes can either rely on the use of special compilers and tools or be transparent to the user.

4.2   Dynamic Concurrency Throttling

We start by presenting the studies that comprise the approaches where the definition of the ideal number of threads to execute a parallel application is performed before the application execution, that is, the approaches that use prediction models. In this case, there is no adaptation of the parallel execution at runtime. Then, we discuss the studies that perform adaptation at runtime and/or are transparent to the programmer/end user.

4.2.1 Approaches with no Runtime Adaptation and no Transparency

In 2001 and 2002, Taylor et al. [118, 119] proposed a model that uses analytical models to predict the performance of three kernels from the NAS Parallel Benchmark (BT, LU, and SP). The model consists of performance coupling, which quantifies the interaction between adjacent kernels in a parallel application, giving more accuracy to the model. Results were validated on a machine with 80 processors, showing that the higher the performance coupling, the better the model accuracy.

Engin et al. [49] refined and adapted a multilayer neural network to predict the performance of parallel applications on two different high-performance platforms (IBM Blue Gene and Intel Itanium 2). The proposed model predicts the performance of SMG2000 application within 5–7% error across a large multidimensional parameter space. However, there is a large overhead due to the time required to gather each data point in the training set. An extended version of the work was published by Karan et al. [107], where two benchmarks were added: a semi-coarsening multigrid solver and LINPACK.

In order to reduce the overhead of performance prediction models, Leo et al. [127] propose an approach that uses partial executions of an application to predict its entire behavior. The idea is to predict the overall execution time of a large-scale application through the execution of a short test drive of the application. Two benchmarks from the ASCI Purple Suite were used to validate the model on ten different multicore platforms. The results show that the proposed model can predict the performance with an accuracy up to 97% or even higher. Moreover, in the best case, it adds an overhead of only 1% on the total execution time.

Bradley et al. [5] explore the use of regression to predict the performance of a larger number of processors through training data obtained from a smaller number of processors. Three techniques are proposed: one that applies a multivariate regression over the execution time from the training step to predict the performance of a larger number of processors, and two other techniques that refine this model by using pre-processor information for handling computation and communication separately. The model was validated by running seven benchmarks from the NAS Parallel Benchmark, and Sweep3d on the Atlas cluster with 1152 four-way AMD Opteron nodes. Results show a prediction error from 6.2% to 17.3%.

A framework for the automatic construction of performance skeletons to predict performance on distributed environments is proposed by Sukhdeep et al. [110]. The approach captures the execution behavior of an application and automatically generates a skeleton of a program that reflects its entire behavior. The framework was validated through the execution of six kernels from the NAS Parallel Benchmarks on a cluster of 10 Intel Xeon dual CPU. Results show that the automatically generated performance skeletons can predict application performance with an average error of 8%.

Sharkawi et al. [106] propose a methodology to predict the performance of HPC applications running on different architectures. The method uses data obtained from the executions on the base machine to predict the performance of other four systems (IBM JS22, p570, ×3550, and ×3650). Basically, benchmarks are executed on the base machine to get application performance metrics, which are correlated with data from the target platform through a genetic algorithm. The model was validated through the execution of the SPEC CFP2006 benchmark suite on the base machine and the target platforms. Results show an average error of 7.2% when the performance is predicted to the same system where the data were collected, and an average error up to 12.8% for different ISAs.

Artificial neural networks (ANNs) were used by Tiwari et al. [120] to predict the power and energy usage for memory and CPU when executing the certain HPC computational kernels. These ANNs were trained using empirical data gathered on the target architecture. The approach was validated running three distinct computational kernels (matrix multiplication, stencil, and LU factorization) on an Intel Xeon E5530 (which has 2 quad-core processors). The results show that, once the networks are trained, they can predict the performance, power and energy consumption for the CPU and memory with a maximum error of 5.5%.

Cabrera et al. [18] propose an analytical model to predict the energy consumption for the high-performance LINPACK running on HPC systems. The proposed approach is based on the performance model presented in Chou et al. [25]. The authors added to the model new parameters regarding the energy required to perform communication and computation. The energy model was validated on a cluster with 24 nodes, each one containing an Intel Xeon dual-core. Results show that the model predicted the energy with 1% of error in the best case. However, it achieved an error of 67% in the worst case.

Song et al. [111] present a unified performance and power model for the NekBone mini-application using a combination of empirical analysis and micro-benchmarking. The approach considers the impact of computation and communication, and quantitatively predicts their impact on both performance and energy consumption. The model was validated on a cluster with 64 nodes, each one with a dual-socket AMD Opteron processor. The results show that the model provides performance and energy prediction with a maximum error of 5% when predicting the behavior for up to 1024 cores.

Considering HPC applications, a model for software estimation of power consumption in an HPC environment is proposed by Witkowski et al. [125]. A multivariate linear regression is used to find out the hardware data with high correlation with power consumption and to build the model. Several benchmarks were used to train and validate the model, such as Abinit, NAMD, Intel LINPACK, HMMER, among others, on three distinct machines: a dual-core Intel Xeon 3.0 GHz; a quad-core Intel Xeon 2.33 GHz; and a dual-core AMD Opteron 2.2 GHz. Results show that the proposed model can predict the power consumption of HPC applications with a maximum error up to 7.88%

An energy prediction mechanism for OpenMP applications using a random forest modeling (RFM) approach in compilers is proposed by Benedict et al. [8].

The approach is expressed in five steps: (1) an analyzer entity does an initial analysis of OpenMP applications regarding parallelism and code regions. (2) The optimizer entity finds the optimal energy solution for the identified code regions considering performance concerns. (3) The optimizer entity prepares a list of the best configurations and submits them to the prediction mechanism. (4) The energy consumption and performance for each configuration are predicted by using the RFM. (5) Finally, the predicted results are sent to the optimizer entity, where it would provide the best solution. The proposed approach was validated by running different OpenMP applications (NAS benchmarks, matrix multiplications, n-body simulations, and stencil applications) on four Intel Xeon E5-4560, each offering 8 cores. From the experiments, the authors observed that RFM predicted the applications almost accurately with R2 (coefficient of determination) of 0.998 in the best case (the closer to 1, the better), and 0.814 in the worst case.

DwarfCode, a performance prediction for hybrid applications, is proposed by Zhang et al. [128]. It uses computation and communication traces to predict the performance of MPI-OpenMP and MPI-ACC applications. DwarfCode captures these traces and generates a shorter benchmark of the entire application which mimics its behavior. Then, this shorter benchmark is executed on the target platform to predict the application's performance. The model was validated running the NAS parallel Benchmarks on three clusters, each with a different number of nodes. Results show that the approach can predict the performance of MPI applications with an error rate lower than 10% for computing and communication-intensive applications.

A prediction framework that matches executions signatures for performance predictions of HPC applications using a single small-scale application execution is proposed by Jayakumar et al. [50]. The framework extracts execution signatures of applications and performs automatic phase identification of different application phases. Then, these signatures are matched with the execution profiles of reference kernels stored in a database and used to predict the performance of the application phases during execution time. To validate the prediction framework, three large-scale real scientific applications (GTC, Sweep3d, and SMG2000) were executed on an 800-core heterogeneous cluster and a 3600-core cluster. The results achieved show that the proposed framework can predict the energy consumption with errors in the range 0.4–18.7%.

4.2.2 Approaches with Runtime Adaptation and/or Transparency

Considering that the CPU availability can change during the execution due to thermal overload and transient errors, Ding et al. [31] study how a parallel execution can cope with changes in the CPU availability. The goal is to decide at runtime the best strategy to employ when the number of CPUs available to an application is changed, considering the energy-delay product. The approach uses performance counters (or data) provided by the architecture and a power model statistic. Based on this information, it decides the ideal number of CPUs, threads, and voltage/frequency levels to use when a variation in the resource availability occurs. The approach was implemented using a full system simulator (Virtutech Simics 3.0) and validated through the execution of two applications: fast Fourier transform and multigrid. Compared to the baseline, in which there is no adaptation in the platform when the available resources change, the approach reduced the EDP up to 83.3%.

Thread Reinforcer [92] is an example of work that presents a certain level of transparency to the user, but cannot adjust the number of threads dynamically, at runtime. It consists of a framework that runs in two steps: (1) the application binary is executed multiple times with a different number of threads for a short period (e.g., 100 ms), while Thread Reinforcer searches for the appropriate configuration. (2) Once this configuration is found, the application is fully re-executed with the number of threads defined in the first step. By executing the application binary already compiled, Thread Reinforcer is a particular case that keeps binary compatibility. However, it works well only for applications that have a short initialization period—thus introducing a small overhead—and it considers that all parallel regions of an application have the same behavior.

The approaches proposed in [55] and [115] already present some adaptability through the definition of the number of threads at runtime. Jung et al. [55] present performance models for generating adaptive parallel code for SMT architectures. In their work, an analysis is applied during compile time to filter parallel loops in OpenMP in which the overhead from the thread management (creation/termination, workload distribution, and synchronization) is higher than its own workload. Then, at runtime, the master thread uses the compilation time analysis to dynamically estimate whether it should use the SMT feature of the processor or not. This approach is also dependent on a compiler and can only be applied for SMT processors.

Suleman et al. propose the feedback-driven threading (FDT) framework [115], which can adapt the number of threads considering contention for locks and memory bandwidth. The framework consists of a specific compiler that samples a portion of parallel regions of an application implemented with OpenMP, inserts instructions at the entry and exit of the critical section, and executes it sequentially to analyze synchronization and communication points. It then uses this analysis to estimate the optimal number of threads for the given parallel region. The application is executed with the estimated number of threads and cannot readapt at runtime. Furthermore, FDT considers that all threads are homogeneous and ignores fundamental hardware characteristics that are highly correlated to the parallel application behavior: FDT assumes that bandwidth requirement increases linearly with the number of threads, ignoring cache contention and data-sharing between the threads. Moreover, FDT does not consider the effects of the SMT feature (discussed in Sect. 1.2), by assuming that only one thread executes per core.

More adaptive solutions, which consider runtime and continuous adaptation, include [3, 20, 28, 29, 63, 91, 96]. However, these solutions rely on (i) support from hardware/OS or a special compiler/tool; and (ii) the need for recompilation or a previous offline analysis, as discussed next.

In [28], Curtis-Maury et al. propose a framework for nearly optimal online adaptation of multithreaded code for low-power and high-performance execution. The approach has an offline phase in which data from hardware counters are collected, and profiles of parallel execution are analyzed. Then, at runtime, the framework uses the information obtained in the offline phase to adapt the number of threads and achieve optimal performance or energy consumption. A solution proposed by Curtis-Maury et al. is ACTOR [29], a system that dynamically changes the number of threads to improve energy efficiency. ACTOR is divided into three steps: (1) artificial neural networks (ANNs) are trained offline to model the relationship between performance counter events and the resulting performance with a different number of threads; (2) at runtime, the derived ANN models are used to predict the performance of parallel regions that were previously identified by the programmer with special function calls from the ACTOR library; (3) the parallel regions are executed with the predicted number of threads. Although the number of threads is predicted at runtime in [28] and [29], an offline phase is required before the execution of each parallel application. Therefore, if either the input set or processor is changed, the offline analysis must be re-executed, which significantly increases the total execution time of the entire framework.

Thread Tailor [63] is a framework that dynamically adjusts the number of threads to optimize system efficiency, such as cache and memory space. The approach works as follows: (1) programmers create a parallel application that uses a high number of threads; (2) the binary created is profiled offline to collect statistics regarding the number of threads, communication, and synchronization to form a communication graph; (3) at runtime, a dynamic compiler takes a quick snapshot of the system state to determine how many free resources are available and to decide the optimum number of threads; (4) based on that information, the dynamic compiler generates code for the new threads, intercepts future calls to thread creations, and redirects them to the new threads. However, as Thread Tailor works for PThreads and MPI, it requires huge effort from the programmer to develop a parallel application that is able to use a high number of threads/processes, since the developer must explicitly implement thread/process management (creation/termination), workload distribution, synchronization and communication points between threads/processes.

Parcae [96] is a framework that comprises a compiler and runtime system to optimize the overall system performance. The compiler (Nona) identifies paralleliz-able regions in a sequential program and applies multiple parallelizing transforms (data-parallel with critical sections and a pipeline transform) to each region. When the application is executing, the Parcae runtime system (Decima monitor and the Morta executor) monitors the program performance and system events to determine the best configuration for the parallel application. However, Parcae relies on system support (compiler, monitor, and executor) to modify sequential applications at compilation and execution time. Therefore, if there are any changes in the environment (input set or microarchitecture), the application needs to be recompiled.

Porterfield et al. [91] propose an adaptive runtime system that automatically adjusts the number of threads based on online measurements of system resource usage. The approach extends Qthreads (a parallel library [123]) to be used with MAESTRO, a dynamic runtime library for power and concurrency adaptation of parallel applications [90]. However, it is dependent on ROSE source-to-source compiler [93] to obtain OpenMP directives and map the functions and data structures to the Qthreads library. OpenMPE [3] is an extension designed for energy management of OpenMP applications, in which the programmers expose energy saving opportunities through the insertion of directives in OpenMP codes. However, it works only for the Insieme compiler and runtime system from the Insieme Project [53].

Based on a combination of Amdahl's law with regression analysis, Ju et al. [54] propose a model to estimate the optimal number of threads for heterogeneous many-core systems. The model considers information obtained from a prediction model to dynamically adjust the number of threads and processing cores at runtime. The model was validated by executing applications from the PARSEC suite on a heterogeneous system consisting of one Intel Xeon Phi Coprocessor and Xeon E5-2670 CPU. Compared to the traditional way that parallel applications are executed on heterogeneous systems, the proposed model improved the performance up to 48.6% and reduced the energy up to 59%.

More transparent approaches, which do not need support from special compilers, include [72, 112, 113]. In Srinath et al. [112], ParallelismDial (PD), a model that automatically tunes a program's performance to the underlying system is proposed. It monitors the system efficiency, regulates the degree of parallelism, and continuously adapts the execution through a heuristic to an optimum point of operation. The heuristic used to find the best degree of parallelism is based on the hill-climbing search algorithm, which works as follows: (1) the parallel region runs with only one thread to establish a sequential measure; (2) the same region is executed with three degrees of parallelism (low, medium, and high); (3) the search is refined to the best interval and continues until the optimum point be reached.

In Srinath et al. [113], ParallelismDial was extended to Varuna system. It comprises two components: (1) an analytical engine which continuously monitors changes in the system using hardware performance counters, models the execution behavior, and determines the optimum degree of parallelism; and (2) a manager that automatically regulates the execution to match the degree of parallelism determined by the analytical engine. PD and Varuna comprise a monitor system that intercepts thread and task creation from PThreads, TBB, and Prometheus libraries, and create a pool of tasks to optimize their degree of parallelism. However, to do so efficiently, PD and Varuna create a large number of fine-grained tasks. Consequently, it requires more effort from the programmer, that is, the programmer is required to create as many threads as possible, each one with the lowest possible workload. Because of this intrinsic characteristic, PD and Varuna focus on recursive applications that are mostly concentrated on big data. Besides that, they cannot optimize

OpenMP applications due to limitations of the system (virtual tasks) used to control parallelism [1]. Finally, LAANT [72] is a library that automatically adjusts the number of threads of OpenMP applications. In this approach, code must be modified by the programmer to include additional function calls in each parallel region of interest in the application.

4.3 Dynamic Voltage and Frequency Scaling

4.3.1 Approaches with no Runtime Adaptation and no Transparency

Snowdon et al. [109] and [108] propose a model to predict performance and energy under different DVFS levels. Given a workload execution at one frequency setpoint, the model predicts the runtime and energy at any other CPU frequency setpoint. The model consists of three steps: (1) data sets are generated to calibrate the model using least-squares linear regression; (2) the model is validated through comparison with the measured power and performance; (3) the model is built to predict performance and energy. Results were validated through the execution of different applications from the MiBench suite, SPEC CINT95, and elsewhere on a PXA255 processor, based on an ARMv5T-compatible XScale core. The maximum error for performance prediction was 3.7%, and the average error was 0.72%. As for energy prediction, the maximum error was 4.9%, and the average error was 1.5%.

Rountree et al. [100] present an analytic framework to predict the applications performance under different DVFS configurations. The framework is processor-independent and uses a single performance counter, namely Leading Loads. The approach was validated through the execution of different kernels from the NAS Parallel Benchmarks and SPEC CPU benchmarks, and the results show improvements concerning the accuracy compared to the existing approaches. Mifakhutdinov et al. [81] propose a DVFS performance predictor for realistic memory systems. The framework, CRIT+BW, considers two variables when predicting the memory performance: memory access latency and effects of prefetching. CRIT+BW was evaluated using two different application classes from SPEC 2006 benchmarks: memory-intensive and prefetch-heavy. Results show that when CRIT+BW is used together with DVFS, energy consumption can be saved by up to 65% when compared to the execution without DVFS and CRIT+BW, while previously DVFS approaches were able to reduce the energy consumption by less than 34%.

Rossi et al. [99] propose an offline approach based on a multiple linear regression model that estimates the power consumption for different DVFS policies: *performance*, *ondemand*, and *powersave*. Then, the programmer can use the predicted values to select the DVFS policy that provides the lowest power consumption. Marques et al. [33] perform an extensive study addressing multidimensional frequency scaling for multicore embedded systems. Different hardware components were evaluated and had the operating frequency changed, such as processor, L2 cache, and RAM. The main idea is to find the combination of frequency for each hardware component that delivers the lowest energy consumption and EDP when running parallel applications. Results showed that by selecting the ideal configuration before the application execution, it is possible to improve the EDP by up to 46.4% when compared to the standard way that frequencies are configured.

4.3.2 Approaches with Runtime Adaptation and/or Transparency

A power-aware algorithm that automatically and transparently adapts CPU voltage and frequency to reduce energy consumption with minimal impact on performance is proposed by Hsu and Feng [46]. The algorithm schedules CPU frequency in such a way that energy savings are obtained with a performance slowdown lower than the maximum provided by the user. At every second, the algorithm analyzes the actual power consumption and takes decisions regarding the ideal CPU frequency. To validate the proposed algorithm, different applications from the NAS Parallel Benchmark and SPEC suite were executed on an AMD Athlon64 processor and on an Opteron-based cluster with four quad-cores. Compared to the application's execution without changing the CPU frequency, the proposed algorithm reduced the energy consumption up to 25% at the cost up to 5% on performance degradation.

Hotta et al. [45] propose PowerWatch, a power-performance optimization model that adapts the processor frequency at runtime but relies on an offline phase. In the approach, a parallel application is split into several regions by the programmer. Then, each region is executed with different processor frequencies during the offline phase. Finally, the optimization algorithm determines the best processor operating frequency for each region and will rerun the application with such frequency values. Another hybrid approach is the Pack & Cap [27], which manages the CPU voltage–frequency setting and the use of thread affinity (but does not perform Thread Throttling) to optimize performance within a power budget. It consists of an offline phase where a large volume of data (performance, energy, temperature) are collected to train a multinomial logistic regression (MLR) classifier. Then, at runtime, the MLR classifier selects the optimal configuration to execute the rest of the application.

Runtime approaches, which do not need offline analysis but need special compilers/tools to enable the runtime adaptation, are discussed next. DEP+BURST[2] is an online DVFS performance predictor to manage multithreaded applications that run on top of the Java virtual machine. Wu et al. [126] propose a dynamic compiler system that interacts with the application during execution to reduce energy consumption by applying different DVFS schemes. Hsu and Feng [46] propose PART, an automatic power-aware runtime system that adapts the CPU operating frequency in order to reduce the energy consumption with a minimal performance slowdown.

Next, online and transparent mechanisms are detailed. Rizvandi et al. [98] propose a maximum-minimum-frequency DVFS algorithm (MMF-DVFS). It uses a linear combination of the maximum and minimum processor frequencies that reduce the energy consumption with minimal impact on the system's performance. Ge et al. [37] present the CPU Management Infra-Structure for Energy Reduction (CPU-MISER), a runtime DVFS scheduler for multicore-based power-aware clusters. It consists of a monitor that collects performance events from the application using hardware counters and predicts the application's workload based on the predicted value, the DVFS scheduler to determine the CPU frequency for the rest of the application. Miftakhutdinov [82] proposes a performance predictor to control the CPU frequency level at runtime. The model measures the workload characteristics for each parallel region and estimates the performance at different CPU frequency levels. Then, when the region is re-executed, the CPU frequency is set to the level that offers the best performance. Chen et al. [24] propose a model with the same purpose, but to predict the best CPU frequency level and voltage for multicore embedded systems, aiming to reduce the energy consumption. In the approach, the user must define a given performance loss factor so the model can reduce the energy consumption accordingly.

4.4 DCT and DVFS

4.4.1 Approaches with no Runtime Adaptation and no Transparency

Abhishek and Margaret [11] propose a thread criticality predictor for parallel applications. The main idea is to predict the slowest thread of an application, disable such thread, or adjust the operating frequency of the processor, and then redistribute the workload among the remaining threads. The model was validated on an ARM-based-in-order (32 cores) simulator running benchmarks from the SPLASH-2 and PARSEC suite. Results show that the approach can improve the performance up to 31.8% and reduce energy consumption by 15% on average, when compared to the execution without the approach.

The work developed by Basmadjian and Meer [6] presents a methodology for estimating the dynamic power consumption of multicore processors. The proposed mathematical model considers different components, such as chip-level (frequency and voltage), inter-die communication (active cores and dies involved in the communication/computation), and die-level (cores and off-chip caches). The authors also consider the impact of DVFS on the energy consumption. Two synthetic benchmarks were executed on Intel and AMD multicore processors to validate the approach. Results show that the model provides an accuracy within a maximum error of 5% when predicting the energy consumption of a parallel application.

A technique to predict the number of threads and DVFS level that offers the best performance and energy consumption for parallel applications is proposed by Sensi et al. [101]. The idea is to execute the program using few configurations and then predict the behavior of the other settings through multiple linear regression. The proposed technique was validated by executing the PARSEC benchmark on a machine with 24 cores and 13 possible CPU frequency levels. The results show that performance and power consumption can be predicted with an average of 96% of accuracy by executing only 1% of the total possible configurations.

4.4.2   Approaches with Runtime Adaptation and/or Transparency

Li and Martinez [67] investigate techniques to reduce the energy consumption of parallel applications under given performance restrictions. The proposed approach takes place in the possible number of active processors and different CPU frequency levels available. Because many parallel applications are generally not written to change the number of processors at runtime, the authors approximate the behavior by simulating the technique in two phases: (1) each application is executed once for every combination of the processor number and DVFS level, and collect the energy and performance for each instance of the parallel region. (2) The authors simulated different optimization mechanisms with Matlab to find the combination of the processor number and DVFS level that offers the best results. To validate the technique, the authors simulated a 16-processor CMP and executed six applications. The authors concluded that for a parallel region and a performance target, the choice of operating points that minimize power consumption is nontrivial.

In order to address the gap between power and parallelism in processors versus memory system, Porterfield et al. [90] propose MAESTRO. It is a dynamic runtime power and concurrency adaptation of parallel applications. MAESTRO was designed to run within the application's address space and communicate directly with the application and thread scheduling. When MAESTRO detects the memory is saturated, it reduces the pressure on memory either by slowing all the cores through DVFS or by turning off a subset of cores. To incorporate the functionalities of MAESTRO on applications and to dynamically adapt DVFS and number of cores, an API threading interface has been created. Experimental evaluations were performed on an AMD Phenom processor running five applications from the NAS Parallel Benchmark. Compared to the execution without DVFS and number of cores adaptation, MAESTRO reduced the power consumption up to 9.5%.

Li et al. [65] propose a library to save energy with no performance loss for hybrid MPI/OpenMP applications. The library has an offline phase to train a model that will be used at runtime to determine the ideal configuration (number of threads and CPU frequency) for each OpenMP region. Seven applications from the NAS Parallel Benchmarks were executed on a cluster with three different node architectures. The results show a high accuracy of the model in all cases: more than 75% of the samples have less than 10% error. Moreover, the proposed model yields substantial energy savings (4.18% on average and up to 13.8%) with negligible performance loss. In order to use this library, the user has to instrument the applications with functions calls around each OpenMP region and selected MPI operations (collectives and MPI_Waitall). Although this library does not require special compiler/tools, the user needs to modify and recompile the source code, in addition to having prior knowledge of MPI functions. Also, if the user wants to use another processor, it is necessary to rerun the entire training set.

LIMO [20] is a dynamic system that monitors the application at runtime, being able to adapt the execution accordingly. However, this solution requires hardware modifications to determine the working set size of a thread, as well as additional operating system support for detecting threads that block due to busy-wait (spin loop). Consequently, it cannot be applied to any existing commercial microarchitecture. Also, LIMO relies on compiler support to insert special system calls and to modify loop bodies. Therefore, applications need to be recompiled to take advantage of LIMO functionalities.

Li et al. [66] present different models based on statistical analysis to estimate the application power and execution time under different concurrency and CPU frequency configurations. The approach uses static information to get the number of threads and CPU frequency that offers the best results. Then, during the execution, an algorithm adjusts the number of threads and CPU frequency to improve the performance or reduce energy consumption. Applications from the NAS Parallel Benchmark MZ and the ASC Sequoia codes were executed on two nodes, each with four AMD Opteron quad-core processors. Compared to the execution with four processors and four cores per processor, running at the highest processor frequency, the proposed model reduced the energy consumption up to 13.8% with negligible performance loss.

Hwang and Chung [48] propose a dynamic power management technique for reducing the energy consumption of multicore-based embedded mobile devices. The idea is to define at runtime the appropriate number of active cores to execute each phase of the program. As an example, when the application execution enters in a serial region, only one core is computing, then, all the other cores can be tuned off to save energy. The approach works only for OpenMP 2.0 and depends on the *OMPi*, a portable C compiler for OpenMP V2.0 [30]. In order to define which cores will be turned off and at what time of the execution it will occur, directives of the power management library are inserted into the OpenMP code during the compilation by the *OMPi* compiler. The proposed system was validated on two multicore processors (Intel Quad core and an ARM-11 MPCore) running eight programs from the NAS Parallel Benchmark. As the applications from the NAS are highly parallel, the authors intentionally added serial functions in the programs to increase the serial portions of the benchmark. Compared to the DVFS technique, the proposed approach can reduce the power consumption by 18% on average.

Two adaptive techniques to reduce the energy consumption through resource management on multicore processors are introduced in Hankendi and Coskun [42]. The first technique dynamically packs the active threads onto a variable number of cores and jointly uses DVFS to optimize performance while meeting the power constraints. In the other one, an adaptive resource allocation strategy to improve the energy efficiency is proposed. The two techniques require static information obtained from a multinomial logistic regression model. The input of the model are functions of the system performance counter values, per-core temperatures, and the current operating point. The output is the optimal configuration, which is accessed in the form of a lookup table during execution. The PARSEC benchmark was used to train the regression model and validate the proposed model. Executions were performed on an AMD 12-core server which comprises two 6 core. Compared to the state of the art, the first technique reduced the energy consumption by 51.6%, while the second one improved the energy efficiency by 17%.

In Alessi et al. [3], an extension for OpenMP (OpenMPE) designed for energy management is presented. The approach allows programmers to expose energy saving opportunities through (1) characterizing application behavior by providing a semantic region structure; (2) setting per-code region multi-objective goals and constraints; (3) exposing application-level tunable parameters. OpenMPE exploits DVFS, they adjust the number of threads and application-level content adaptation. OpenMPE works only for the Insieme compiler and runtime system from the Insieme Project. The approach was validated through the execution of a video decoder application on an ARM big.LITTLE architecture comprising a Cortex-A15 and a Cortex-A7, and on an Intel i7 quad-core. Compared to the Linux ondemand governor, OpenMPE saved up to 77% and 31% of energy on the mobile and general-purpose platform, respectively.

Shafik et al. [104] propose an adaptive and scalable energy minimization model for OpenMP programs, which comprises two steps: (1) code annotations are inserted by the programmer in the sequential and parallel parts of the code to enable energy minimization with specified performance requirements; (2) the runtime system reads these performance requirements and uses this information to guide the energy minimization. The same method, but aiming to improve lifetime reliability through balanced thermal controls while meeting a given power budget, was presented by Shafik et al. in [105].

Nornir [102] is a runtime system that monitors the application execution and adjusts the resources configurations (DVFS, number of threads, and thread placement) in order to satisfy either performance or power consumption requirements. To use Nornir, the user has to install a system to manage the features provided by the OS (e.g., DVFS management and energy profiling), and instrument the parallel programming framework with Nornir functions. Marathe et al. [77] propose *Conductor*, a runtime system that dynamically selects the ideal number of threads and DVFS state to improve performance under a power constraint for hybrid applications (MPI + OpenMP). First the application is monitored in order to gauge its representative behavior, and then, a local search algorithm is applied to find and select the configuration to reduce power with minimal impact on execution time. For that, Conductor needs code modifications to insert functions.

Chapter 5
Case Study: DCT with Aurora

5.1 The Need for Adaptability and Transparency

Figure 5.1a shows the usual way of finding the best number of threads to run a parallel application [68, 70, 71]. First, the source code is compiled and executed n times with a different number of threads, where n is the number of available cores in the processor microarchitecture. In this phase, one also has to consider that each application may contain p parallel regions, in which each region can be better executed with a different number of threads. Therefore, the search space corresponds to the execution of n^p combinations of number of threads for each application, where p is greater or equal to 1. After the offline training period, the best configuration is selected, and the next executions will be performed with the configuration found in this step.

In order to understand the huge design space exploration concerning the selection of the ideal number of threads to run a parallel application, let us consider an application with 5 parallel regions running on a 32 multicore processor. In such a case, there will be 32^5 possible combinations, which results in *33,554,432* executions before selecting the ideal configuration. Supposing that each execution would spend 1 min (60 s), it would be necessary approximately 65 days to find the best configuration. However, if there is any change in the application behavior (e.g., input set size) or the execution environment, the executions must be performed again.

Therefore, Aurora was developed to cope with the challenge of selecting the best number of threads to execute each parallel region of an OpenMP application [73]. It automatically finds, at runtime and according to a given metric defined a priori by the user, the ideal number of threads for each parallel region of any OpenMP application. Moreover, it can also readapt according to a change in the behavior of a particular parallel region during program execution. Because of its dynamic adaptability, Aurora deals with the intrinsic characteristics of the application as well as the microarchitecture on which it will execute; it also takes into account

A. Francisco Lorenzon, A. C. S. Beck Filho, *Parallel Computing Hits the Power Wall*, SpringerBriefs in Computer Science, https://doi.org/10.1007/978-3-030-28719-1_5

Fig. 5.1 Adaptation of
OpenMP applications. (**a**)
Brute force. (**b**) Aurora

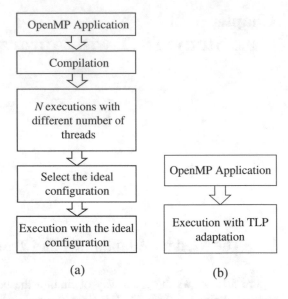

(a)   (b)

the current input set and application changes at runtime, resulting in significant
performance and energy improvements.

Aurora was built on top of the original OpenMP library and is completely transparent to both designer and end user. Given an OpenMP application binary, Aurora
runs on it without any code changes. Therefore, existing OpenMP applications do
not need to be annotated, recompiled, or pass through any code transformation.
Such transparency is achieved by redirecting the calls originally targeted for the
dynamically linked OpenMP library to Aurora. This retargeting is configured by
simply setting an environment variable in the Operating System.

5.2   Aurora: Seamless Optimization of OpenMP Applications

5.2.1   Integration to OpenMP

As already described in Chap. 2.1.2, parallelism in OpenMP is exploited through
the insertion of directives in the sequential code that inform the compiler how and
which parts of the application should be executed in parallel [22]. OpenMP provides
three ways for exploiting parallelism: parallel loops, sections, and tasks. Parallel
sections and tasks are only used in very particular cases: when the programmer must
distribute the workload over the threads in a similar way as PThreads, and when the
application uses recursion (i.e., sort algorithms), respectively. On the other hand,
parallel loops are used to parallelize applications that work on multidimensional
data structures (i.e., array, grid, etc.), so the loop iterations (*for*) can be split into
multithread executions. Therefore, parallel loops are by far the most used approach

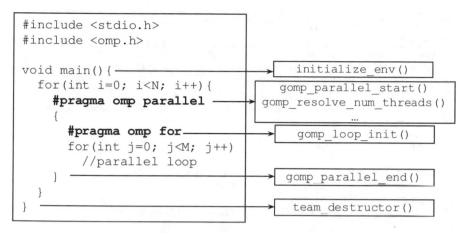

Fig. 5.2 OpenMP execution environment with the respective *libgomp* functions

(all the aforementioned benchmark sets are implemented in this way). For now, Aurora works to optimize parallel loops and does not influence in any way other OpenMP applications that are parallelized using sections or tasks.

All functionalities provided by OpenMP are implemented into the *libgomp*, a GNU Offloading and Multi-Processing Runtime Library. This library is dynamically linked to applications that use OpenMP, so any modifications in its code are completely transparent to user applications. Aurora was incorporated into this library. In order to better understand how Aurora works, let us first consider Fig. 5.2, which illustrates the regular way for parallelizing an iterative application with parallel loops [22] and the respective main functions implemented by *libgomp*. When the program starts executing, the *initialize_env()* function is called, which is responsible for initializing all the environment variables used by OpenMP during the application execution. When the program reaches the directive *#pragma omp parallel* (used to indicate a parallel region), functions to create and define the number of threads (*gomp_resolve_num_threads()*) are called. Within the parallel region, the directive *#pragma omp for* indicates the loop that must be parallelized. At the end of the parallel region, the function *gomp_parallel_end()* joins the threads and finalizes the parallel region environment. Finally, when the application ends, *team_destructor()* concludes the entire OpenMP environment.

Aurora functionalities were split into four functions (discussed in details next). They were incorporated into the *libgomp* functions previously mentioned. Algorithm 1 depicts the modifications done in the source code of each function in order to support Aurora functions. *libgomp* also has another function called *gomp_loop_init()*, which was not modified as its job is to distribute the workload between the already defined threads.

auroraInitEnv() is responsible for recognizing the Aurora optimization target defined by the environment variable (OMP_AURORA) and for initializing the necessary data structures, libraries, and variables used to control the search

---

Algorithm 1 OpenMP functions that were modified to integrate Aurora optimization

---

 1: **function** INITIALIZE_ENV($void$)
 2:     Initialization of OpenMP environment (variables, CPU affinity, wait policy, etc.)
 3:     **if** OMP_AURORA is $defined$ **then**
 4:         $aurora\_metric \leftarrow$ get the value defined by the user in OMP_AURORA
 5:         $aurora\_start\_search \leftarrow$ get the value defined by the user in $AURORA\_START$
 6:         auroraInitEnv($aurora\_metric$, $aurora\_start\_search$)
 7:     **end if**
 8: **end function**

 9: **function** GOMP_PARALLEL_START($*fn$, $*data$, $num\_threads$)
10:     $ptrToRegion \leftarrow$ gets pointer to fn address region
11:     **if** $Aurora$ is $Enabled$ **then**
12:         $num\_threads \leftarrow$ auroraResolveNumThreads($ptrToRegion$)
13:     **else**
14:         $num\_threads \leftarrow$ gomp_resolve_num_threads($num\_threads$, 0)
15:     **end if**
16:     gomp_team_start(fn, $data$, $num\_threads$, 0, gomp_new_team($num\_threads$))
17: **end function**

18: **function** GOMP_PARALLEL_END($void$)
19:     **if** OMP_AURORA is $defined$ **then**
20:         auroraEndParallelRegion();
21:     **end if**
22:     finalize parallel region environment
23:     $gomp\_team\_end()$
24: **end function**

25: **function** TEAM_DESTRUCTOR($void$)
26:     **if** OMP_AURORA is $defined$ **then**
27:         auroradestructEnv();
28:     **end if**
29:     $pthread\_key\_delete(gomp\_thread\_destructor)$
30: **end function**

---

algorithm (described in Chap. 5.2.2). The pseudocode of this function can be seen in Algorithm 2. ***auroraInitEnv*** is called from the original *initialize_env()* only if Aurora optimization is enabled, as presented in lines 3–7 in Algorithm 1. If OMP_AURORA is not defined, the OpenMP execution follows its standard behavior.

***auroraResolveNumThreads*()** sets the number of threads that execute each parallel region based on the current state of the search algorithm. Also, it initializes the counters for collecting data from the execution environment of the current parallel region. Algorithm 3 depicts the pseudocode of this function: if the parallel region is a new region, the search algorithm will start the search from the initial state (*S0*) and with the number of threads defined either by the environment variable AURORA_START or by 2 that is the standard value used by Aurora. Also, if the search algorithm is in the *END* state, the best number of threads (*bnt*) found to

---

Algorithm 2 Initialization of Aurora environment

1: **function** AURORAINITENV(*metric, startSearch*)
2:     *numCores* ← get the total number of cores through *sysconf*
3:     *threadStartSearch* ← get the number of threads defined to start the search
4:     Initialize hardware counters to get the parallel region behavior
5:     **for** *i* in *maxNumberOfParallelRegions* **do**
6:         Initialize the variables used to monitor/control the parallel region *i*
7:             i.e., *startSearch, metric, actualstate*
8:     **end for**
9: **end function**

---

execute a parallel region is returned. Otherwise, the actual number of threads (*ant*) is returned. ***auroraResolveNumThreads*** is called by the *gomp_parallel_start()*[1] when Aurora is active, replacing the original *gomp_resolve_num_threads()* function, as depicted in Algorithm 1.

Algorithm 3 Setting up the number of threads

1: **function** AURORARESOLVENUMTHREADS(*ptrToRegion*)
2:     *idR* ← get the id of the parallel region from *ptrToRegion*
3:     **if** *idR* is a *newRegion* **then**
4:         *auroraKernel[idR].state* ← *S0*
5:     **end if**
6:     **switch** *auroraKernel[idR].state* **do**
7:         start monitoring the parallel region behavior
8:         **case** *END*
9:             **return** *auroraKernel[idR].bnt*
10:        **case** *Default*
11:            **return** *auroraKernel[idR].ant*
12: **end function**

***auroraEndParallelRegion*()** is executed after the parallel region to get its execution time, energy, or EDP, depending on the optimization metric defined by the user. Execution time is extracted by the *omp_get_wtime()* function, provided by OpenMP, while energy is obtained directly from the hardware counters present in modern processors. In the case of Intel processors, the running average power limit (RAPL) library is used to get energy and power consumption of CPU-level components [40], while the APM library is used for AMD processors [39]. Such functions and libraries were incorporated to Aurora, being totally transparent to the user. That is, there is no need to make any modifications in the Operating System (package installation, kernel recompilation, etc.) to use them.

---

[1]*GOMP_parallel_start* is also named as *GOMP_parallel*.

Using either one of the objectives of execution time, energy, or EDP, *auroraEnd-ParallelRegion*() performs one step of the search algorithm (which is explained in the next subsection) and, according to this algorithm, it defines the number of threads that will be used for the execution of this parallel region in the next iteration. *auroraEndParallelRegion*() is implemented inside *gomp_parallel_end*() function, and it is called when Aurora is active, as depicted in Algorithm 1.

auroraDestructEnv() concludes and destroys Aurora environment at the end of application execution, when Aurora is active (Algorithm 1). It was implemented inside *team_destructor*() OpenMP function.

To use Aurora, the user simply has to replace the original OpenMP *libgomp* with Aurora's *libgomp*. This new library includes all original OpenMP functionalities plus the new functions of Aurora. When the environment variable *OMP_AURORA* is set in the Linux Operating System, the thread management system of Aurora is used instead of the original OpenMP functions. This environment variable can be configured to the following values (and, therefore, optimization metrics): performance, energy, or EDP. If the variable is not set, Aurora will not influence the execution of that OpenMP application (i.e., the application executes with the original OpenMP functions). In this way, any existing binary code can benefit from Aurora without any modifications or need for recompilation.

5.2.2 Search Algorithm

The heuristic used by Aurora is divided into two phases. The first one investigates the scalability of the parallel region and reduces the size of the space exploration, exponentially increasing the number of threads (i.e., 2, 4, 8, 16, . . .) while there are potential improvements (states *Initial*, *Doubling*, and *Exponential* in Algorithm 4, Fig. 5.3, and Table 5.1). The second phase performs a hill-climbing based algorithm in the interval of threads defined in the first phase (states *Exponential*, *Search*, and *Lateral*). Intuitively, finding the optimal number of threads to execute any parallel region is a convex optimization problem. In this specific problem, it means that there will be only one specific number of thread that delivers the best result for a given metric and parallel region. Hill-climbing algorithms are very suitable for such problems and are also known for having low complexity and being fast, which is essential to reduce the technique overhead (since it is executed at runtime). Other authors have already shown that when hill-climbing is used along with another approach to guide the search, in most cases such algorithms will reach a near-ideal solution, escaping from the local minima and plateaus [52, 116]. As the search algorithm implemented by Aurora learns towards the best number of threads during application execution, all the computation done in the search phase is not wasted (i.e., it is used by the application), reducing the overhead of Aurora.

Algorithm 4 Search algorithm implemented by Aurora

1: **function** SEARCHALGORITHM()
2:     **if** $state \neq END$ **then**
3:         $metricMsmt \leftarrow$ get time, energy, or EDP according to the target metric
4:         **switch** $state$ **do**
5:             **case** $Initial$:
6:                 $lastNT \leftarrow currentNT \leftarrow threadStartSearch$;
7:                 $state \leftarrow Doubling$;
8:             **case** $Doubling$:
9:                 $bestMetricMsmt \leftarrow metricMsmt$;
10:                 $bestNT \leftarrow currentNT$;
11:                 $currentNT \leftarrow currentNT \times 2$;
12:                 $state \leftarrow Exponential$;
13:             **case** $Exponential$:
14:                 $step \leftarrow \frac{lastNT}{2}$;
15:                 **if** $metricMsmt \leq bestMetricMsmt$ **then**
16:                     $bestMetricMsmt \leftarrow metricMsmt$;
17:                     $bestNT \leftarrow currentNT$;
18:                     **if** $currentNT \times 2 \leq numCores$ **then**
19:                         $lt \leftarrow currentNT$;
20:                         $currentNT \leftarrow bestNT \times 2$;
21:                     **else**
22:                         $currentNT \mathrel{-}= step$;
23:                         $state \leftarrow Search$;
24:                     **end if**
25:                 **else**
26:                     **if** $bestNT == \frac{numCores}{2}$ **then**
27:                         $currentNT \mathrel{-}= step$;
28:                     **else**
29:                         $currentNT \mathrel{+}= step$;
30:                     **end if**
31:                     $state \leftarrow Search$;
32:                 **end if**
33:             **case** $Search$:
34:                 **if** $metricMsmt \leq bestMetricMsmt$ **then**
35:                     $bestNT \leftarrow currentNT$;
36:                     $bestMetricMsmt \leftarrow metricMsmt$;
37:                 **end if**
38:                 $step \leftarrow \frac{step}{2}$;
39:                 $currentNT \mathrel{+}= step$;
40:                 **if** $step == 1$ **then**
41:                     $state \leftarrow Lateral$;
42:                 **end if**
43:             **case** $Lateral$:
44:                 **if** $metricMsmt \leq bestMetricMsmt$ **then**
45:                     $bestNT \leftarrow currentNT$;
46:                 **end if**
47:                 Performs lateral movement to avoid minimum locals
48:                 $state \leftarrow END$;
49:     **else**
50:         **if** $workloadVariation == true$ **then**
51:             run Aurora search algorithm again
52:         **end if**
53:     **end if**
54: **end function**

Basically, the algorithm works as follows (Algorithm 4): the search starts by the *Initial* state (*line 5*), where the initial number of threads (*threadStartSearch*) and the current number of threads (*currentNT*) arc defined. Then, the parallel region is executed with the initial number of threads (e.g., 2 threads) and the state changes to

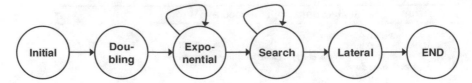

Fig. 5.3 States and transitions of the search algorithm

Table 5.1 States of the search algorithm

State	Operation
Initial	Execution with the initial number of threads
Doubling	Double the number of threads
Exponential	Compare the results achieved in S0 and S1, and exponentially increases the number of threads while either there are improvements or when the max number of hardware threads is met. Then, state changes to Search
Search	Search the ideal number of threads in the interval of candidates defined in S2. When there are only two candidates, state changes to Lateral
Lateral	Define the best number of threads and performs lateral movement
END	Aurora begins to monitor the behavior of the parallel region

Doubling. In this state (*line 8*), the best result so far (*bestMetricMsmt*) is updated with the result obtained by the execution with the number of threads defined in the *Initial* state, the number of threads is doubled, and state changes to *Exponential*. In this state (*line 13*), the measured metric (time, energy, or EDP) is evaluated, and the number of threads continues to double while the measured metric keeps improving and the maximum number of hardware threads available is not reached (*lines 15–32*). Then, the state changes to *Search*. Once in there (*line 33*), Aurora knows the interval of potential candidates for the ideal number of threads, which is in the range between the last number of threads executed and the best number of threads found so far and starts the second phase.

To better understand the second phase, let us consider that the interval of potential candidates lies in the range of 8–16 threads. Then, the algorithm searches for the best number of threads in this range. It will start executing with 12 threads (the average amount between 8 and 16) and then compares to the best result so far to decide the next range (which will be between 8 and 12 or 12 and 16). This process is repeated until the best number of threads is found (state *Search*). After that, state *Lateral* starts, in which lateral movement (*line 47*) is performed to avoid minimal locals and plateaus. This movement is performed by testing a neighboring configuration (number of threads) at another point in the search space that has not yet been tested. When Aurora converges to the best number of threads for a particular parallel region, it begins to monitor the behavior of such region. If there is any change in the workload, which in this work a variation of 30% was considered, the search algorithm starts its execution again.

5.3 Evaluation of Aurora

5.3.1 Methodology

Fifteen applications written in C/C++ and parallelized with OpenMP from assorted benchmarks suites were chosen according to the scalability issues discussed in Sect. 1.2:

- **Seven kernels** from the NAS Parallel Benchmark [4]: *block tri-diagonal solver* (BT), *conjugate gradient* (CG), *discrete 3D fast Fourier transform* (FT), *lower–upper Gauss–Seidel solver* (LU), *multigrid on a sequence of meshes* (MG), *scalar penta-diagonal solver* (SP), and *unstructured adaptive mesh* (UA). As the original version of NAS is written in FORTRAN, the OpenMP-C version developed in [103] is considered.
- **Two applications** from the Rodinia Benchmark Suite [23]: *hotspot* (HS) which iteratively solves a series of differential equations and *streamcluster* (SC), a dense linear algebra algorithm for data mining.
- **Six applications** from different domains: *n-body* (NB)—computes a simulation of a dynamical system of particles [10]; *fast Fourier transform* (FFT)—calculates the discrete Fourier transform of a given sequence [89]; *STREAM* (ST)— measures sustainable memory bandwidth [78]; *Jacobi* (JA) method iteration— computes the solutions of a diagonally dominant system of linear equations [94]. *Poisson* (PO)—computes an approximate solution to the Poisson equation in a rectangular region [94]; and the *high-performance conjugate gradient* benchmark (HPCG), a stand-alone code that measures the performance of basic operations [32].

Two different input sets for each benchmark were considered: small and medium. Table 5.2 depicts the Pearson correlation between each scalability issue (discussed in Chap. 2) and the application. As can be observed, the chosen applications do not scale for different reasons, according to Sect. 1.2. All the data used for the scalability analysis was obtained directly from hardware using Intel Performance Counter Monitor (PCM) [124], Intel Parallel Studio, and Performance Application Programming Interface (PAPI) [15].

As one can note in Fig. 5.4, the chosen benchmarks also cover a wide range of different TLP behaviors. The TLP was measured as defined by the authors in [12]: the average amount of concurrency exhibited by the program during its execution when at least one core is active, and it is expressed in Equation 5.1. c_i is the fraction of time that i cores are concurrently running different threads, n is the number of cores, and $1 - c_0$ is the non-idle time fraction. The closer this value is to 1.0 (normalized to the total number of cores available), the more TLP is available [12].

$$TLP = \frac{\sum_{i=1}^{n} c_i i}{1 - c_0} \tag{5.1}$$

Table 5.2 Pearson correlation between the scalability issues and each benchmark

		NB	FFT	ST	UA	JA	SP	HS	SC	PO	HPCG	MG	BT	LU	CG	FT
Small input	Issue-width saturation	−0.82	−0.71	−0.56	**−0.92**	−0.80	−0.80	**−0.91**	−0.80	−0.84	−0.65	−0.81	−0.75	−0.87	**−0.91**	**−0.90**
	Off-chip bus saturation	0.46	**−0.98**	**−0.90**	−0.84	−0.57	−0.71	−0.51	−0.82	−0.56	**−0.94**	−0.76	−0.79	−0.80	−0.82	−0.68
	Shared memory accesses	0.80	−0.43	−0.71	−0.78	0.52	−0.83	−0.52	**−0.91**	0.71	−0.86	**−0.90**	**−0.91**	**−0.96**	−0.85	−0.78
	Data-synchronization	**0.97**	−0.50	−0.61	−0.49	**0.92**	**0.95**	−0.54	−0.54	**0.94**	−0.24	−0.59	−0.64	−0.61	−0.61	−0.82
Medium input	Issue-width saturation	−0.78	−0.71	−0.63	−0.73	−0.69	−0.82	**−0.92**	−0.76	−0.83	−0.74	−0.79	−0.73	**−0.90**	**−0.94**	**−0.91**
	Off-chip bus saturation	0.39	**−0.97**	**−0.95**	−0.85	**−0.90**	−0.62	−0.52	−0.86	−0.46	**−0.94**	−0.88	−0.79	−0.65	−0.82	−0.76
	Shared memory accesses	0.81	−0.75	−0.73	**−0.94**	0.82	**−0.90**	−0.54	**−0.96**	**−0.94**	−0.86	**−0.96**	**−0.92**	0.09	0.70	−0.86
	Data-synchronization	**0.96**	−0.53	−0.38	−0.74	−0.48	−0.11	−0.64	−0.68	−0.67	−0.70	−0.78	−0.61	−0.18	−0.64	−0.77

Bold values highlight Pearson's correlation of scalability issue that affects each application

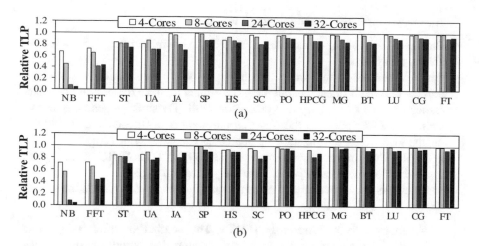

Fig. 5.4 TLP available for each benchmark—normalized w.r.t. the maximum number of threads in each processor. (**a**) Small input set. (**b**) Medium input set

Table 5.3 Main characteristics of each processor

	Intel Core		Intel Xeon	
	i5-4460	i7-6700	E5-2630	E5-2640
Microarchitecture	Haswell	Skylake	Sandy Bridge	Ivy Bridge
# cores	4	4	2×6	2×8
# threads	4	8	24	32
CPU frequency	3.2 GHz	3.4 GHz	2.3 GHz	2.0 GHz
L1 cache	4×32 KB	4×32 KB	12×32 KB	16×32 KB
L2 cache	4×256 KB	4×256 KB	12×256 KB	16×256 KB
L3 cache	6 MB	8 MB	30 MB	40 MB
RAM	16 GB	32 GB	32 GB	64 GB

The closer the TLP value is to 1.0 (normalized to the total number of cores available), the more TLP is available. As an example, NB has the lowest TLP available, where only 10% of the execution is performed in parallel when the 32-core system is considered, while the FT benchmark presents the highest TLP, in which more than 95% of the application is executed in parallel.

The experiments were performed on four different multicore processors (Table 5.3), each one with the Ubuntu Operating System with Kernel v. 4.4.0 in all the machines. The CPU frequency was configured to adjust according to the workload application, using ondemand as DVFS governor, which is the standard governor used in most Linux versions. The applications were compiled with gcc/g++ 6.3, using the optimization flag -O3, and the OpenMP distribution version 4.0. The results presented in the next session are the average of ten executions with a standard deviation lower than 0.5%.

Aurora was evaluated in the following scenarios:

- **Baseline**: the application executes with the maximum number of threads available in the system;
- **OMP_Dynamic**: a built-in feature of OpenMP that dynamically adjusts the number of threads of each parallel region, aiming to make the best use of system resources, such as memory and processor. OMP_Dynamic is generally used to avoid oversubscription, in the way that the number of threads is defined based on the load average utilization of processes on the system [26]. This feature is enabled by using the environment variable OMP_DYNAMIC or through the insertion of the *omp_set_dynamic*() in the source code [22];
- **State-of-the-art approaches**: Aurora was also compared to the most cited approaches in the area:

  - **Feedback-Driven Threading (FDT)**: The number of threads is defined based on the contention for locks and memory bandwidth (as discussed in Sect. 4.2.2) [115].
  - **Varuna**: A high-level comparison with it was performed, by faithfully implementing the Varuna programming model (as defined in [113]) and applying it to the benchmarks.

- **Static Approaches**: in order to measure the efficiency of the search algorithm used by Aurora, two static and offline approaches were implemented:

  - **Oracle Solution**: The execution of each parallel region with the optimal number of threads for each metric, without the cost of the learning curve. The optimal number of threads was obtained through an exhaustive execution of each parallel region of each application with 1 to n threads, where n is the maximum number supported by hardware.
  - **Genetic Algorithm (GA)**: It was implemented to demonstrate how Aurora's hill-climbing fares against such classes of heuristics. GA is a search meta-heuristic based on natural selection and genetics. It uses a concept of a population, which is a set of individual solutions (chromosomes), that can evolve to an optimum solution through generations.

5.3.2 Results

We start by discussing how Aurora handles the scalability issues discussed in Sect. 1.2: off-chip bus saturation, shared memory accesses, data-synchronization, and issue-width saturation. Then, we present a comparison between Aurora and the following executions in Sect. 5.3.2.2: baseline, OMP_Dynamic, FDT, and Varuna, while Sect. 5.3.2.3 compares Aurora to the results achieved by the genetic algorithm. Section 5.3.2.4 discusses the efficiency of the search algorithm implemented by Aurora through the comparison to the Oracle solution. Finally, Sect. 5.3.2.5 draws the limitations of Aurora at this time.

5.3.2.1 Handling Scalability

As a result of its runtime analysis, the search algorithm used by Aurora can detect the point in which the number of threads saturates any metric. As a first example, let us consider the off-chip bus saturation (as discussed in Sect. 1.2) and the execution of HPCG with medium input set on the 24-core system. This benchmark has two main parallel regions that are better executed with a different number of threads (Table 5.4) each. Figure 5.5a shows that when the second region is executed with more than 12 threads, the off-chip bus saturates (100% of utilization), and no further EDP improvements are achieved. By using its continuous monitoring and avoiding this saturation, Aurora was able to reduce the EDP of the whole application by 15% when compared to the baseline execution (24 threads). The very same behavior can be observed in FFT and ST (regardless of the input set) and JA for the medium input set (Table 5.2), but at different improvement ratios.

In applications with high communication demands, there is an optimal point in which the overhead imposed by the shared memory accesses does not overcome the gains achieved by the parallelism exploitation, as discussed in Sect. 1.2. Aurora detected this point for all benchmarks in this class: SC, MG, and BT; LU (with small input); PO, UA, and SP (with medium input) (Table 5.2). For instance, let us consider the SP benchmark running on the 24-core system. This application has nine main parallel regions, in which each one is better executed with a different number of threads. Figure 5.5b shows that when the number of shared memory accesses from all threads in the first parallel region starts to increase (after six threads—primary y-axis), no further improvements in the EDP are achieved (secondary y-axis). As shown in the same figure and Table 5.4, Aurora found the best number of threads to execute this parallel region, providing EDP gains of 58% when compared to the baseline execution (24 threads).

Aurora similarly detects the point where the synchronization time overlaps the gains provided by TLP exploitation. This behavior can be observed in some benchmarks, such as n-body (NB) with small or medium input, or Jacobi(JA) and SP with small input set (Table 5.2). In these benchmarks, the higher the number of threads, the greater the time spent synchronizing, which can worsen the results, as already discussed in Sect. 1.2. The n-body benchmark with the medium input set executing on the 32-core system (Fig. 5.5c) can be discussed as an example. When increasing the number of threads from 1 to 3, performance improves. However, from this point on, the time that the threads spend synchronizing overcomes the gains achieved by the parallelism exploitation (Fig. 5.5c), increasing the energy consumption and EDP of the whole application. As demonstrated in Table 5.4, by avoiding this extra overhead in the synchronization time and setting the right number of threads, Aurora reduced the execution time by 79%, energy by 89%, and EDP by 98%.

Aurora also converges to the best number of threads for applications that are negatively influenced by the issue-width saturation. Some examples are: hotspot (HS), FT, and CG with any input set; and UA and PO with the small input (Table 5.2). Let us consider the hotspot benchmark with the medium input set

Table 5.4 Number of threads found by Aurora

Proc.-#cores		Performance				Energy				EDP			
		4	8	24	32	4	8	24	32	4	8	24	32
NB	S	4	4	4	3	3	3	4	3	3	3	4	3
	M	4	4	4	3	3	3	3	3	4	4	4	3
FFT	S	4	2	4	6	1	1	2	4	2	1	2	4
	M	4	2	6	14	1	1	2	4	2	2	2	4
ST	S	4	2	4	12	1	1	4	4	2	1	4	6
	M	4	2	4	12	1	1	4	4	2	1	4	6
UA	S	4, 4, 4	8, 3, 4	24, 6, 12	32, 11, 14	4, 1, 2	8, 1, 2	24, 6, 4	32, 6, 6	4, 2, 2	8, 1, 2	24, 6, 6	32, 10, 10
		4, 4, 4	8, 8, 8	12, 24, 12	32, 32, 32	4, 4, 4	4, 8, 8	11, 24, 12	32, 32, 32	4, 4, 4	8, 8, 8	24, 12, 12	32, 32, 32
		4, 4, 4	4, 2, 2	12, 6, 6	10, 12, 26	1, 1, 1	2, 1, 1	6, 4, 6	6, 6, 6	1, 1, 1	2, 1, 2	6, 6, 6	6, 6, 6
		4	2	6	10	1	1	4	6	1	2	6	8
	M	4, 4, 4	8, 2, 4	24, 4, 8	32, 11, 14	4, 1, 2	8, 1, 2	24, 2, 4	32, 4, 6	4, 2, 2	8, 1, 2	24, 4, 6	32, 4, 6
		4, 4, 4	8, 8, 8	24, 24, 24	16, 32, 32	4, 4, 4	4, 8, 4	11, 24, 12	13, 32, 14	4, 4, 4	8, 8, 8	24, 24, 12	32, 32, 32
		4, 4, 4	5, 2, 5	6, 4, 11	6, 13, 11	1, 1, 1	1, 1, 1	4, 4, 2	4, 4, 4	2, 2, 2	5, 1, 1	6, 4, 4	6, 4, 4
		4	2	8	12	1	1	2	4	2	1	4	4
JA	S	3	3	12	28	2	2	6	14	2	2	6	15
	M	3	2	10	12	2	2	4	6	2	2	4	6
SP	S	2, 4, 4	2, 2, 4	6, 6, 12	12, 26, 15	2, 1, 3	2, 1, 3	6, 4, 10	6, 4, 13	2, 2, 3	2, 1, 4	6, 4, 12	6, 4, 15
		2, 3, 2	2, 4, 2	6, 12, 6	32, 15, 32	1, 3, 1	1, 3, 1	4, 10, 4	4, 13, 4	2, 3, 2	1, 4, 1	6, 12, 6	4, 15, 4
		3, 3, 4	4, 2, 2	12, 6, 6	15, 6, 8	3, 1, 1	3, 1, 1	10, 4, 2	10, 4, 4	3, 2, 2	3, 1, 1	10, 4, 4	15, 4, 4
	M	3, 4, 2	2, 5, 2	6, 6, 6	12, 10, 10	2, 1, 2	1, 1, 2	4, 4, 6	6, 4, 8	2, 2, 2	2, 1, 2	6, 6, 6	6, 6, 8
		2, 2, 2	2, 2, 5	20, 6, 20	32, 10, 14	1, 2, 1	1, 2, 1	4, 6, 4	4, 8, 4	2, 2, 2	2, 2, 2	6, 6, 6	4, 8, 4
		2, 4, 4	2, 5, 2	6, 6, 24	8, 10, 24	2, 1, 1	2, 1, 1	6, 4, 4	8, 4, 4	2, 2, 2	2, 5, 1	6, 4, 4	8, 6, 4

	S/M												
HS	S	4	4	12	16	4	4	10	16	4	4	12	16
	M	4	4	12	16	4	4	12	16	4	4	12	16
SC	S	4	8	23	9	4	8	7	9	4	8	23	9
	M	4	7	9	15	4	7	7	9	4	7	7	15
PO	S	4	8	12	16	4	8	12	16	4	8	12	16
	M	4	7	12	16	4	3	12	16	4	3	12	16
HPCG	S	4, 4	2, 5	10, 10	8, 30	1, 2	1, 2	4, 6	6, 6	2, 3	2, 2	6, 6	8, 8
	M	–	2, 4	6, 12	8, 32	–	1, 3	4, 8	4, 8	–	2, 3	4, 12	6, 8
MG	S	2, 4	2, 3	6, 8	8, 10	2, 2	2, 2	6, 6	6, 8	2, 3	2, 3	6, 8	8, 8
		3, 3	3, 2	8, 10	10, 12	2, 1	2, 1	6, 4	8, 4	2, 2	3, 2	8, 6	8, 6
	M	4, 4	3, 4	12, 10	16, 16	2, 2	2, 2	4, 6	6, 8	2, 3	2, 3	6, 6	6, 8
BT	S	4, 2	3, 2	8, 10	12, 6	2, 1	2, 1	6, 4	6, 6	3, 2	3, 2	6, 4	8, 6
		2, 4	2, 8	6, 23	10, 28	2, 4	2, 8	6, 22	6, 28	2, 4	2, 8	6, 22	8, 28
	M	4, 4	8, 8	22, 23	31, 30	4, 4	4, 8	22, 22	28, 29	4, 4	8, 8	22, 22	28, 29
LU	S	3, 4	2, 8	8, 24	10, 32	2, 4	1, 8	4, 23	6, 32	2, 4	2, 8	4, 24	8, 32
		4, 4	8, 8	24, 24	32, 32	4, 4	8, 8	23, 23	32, 32	4, 4	8, 8	23, 23	32, 32
	M	4, 4	8, 8	22, 22	27, 31	4, 3	4, 8	10, 22	10, 15	4, 4	8, 8	22, 22	14, 26
CG	S	4, 4	8, 4	12, 24	14, 32	4, 2	4, 2	10, 24	10, 32	4, 3	4, 3	12, 24	14, 32
		4, 4	8, 8	24, 24	32, 32	4, 4	3, 8	24, 12	16, 16	4, 4	8, 8	24, 24	32, 16
	M	4, 4	8, 8	24, 24	31, 32	4, 4	8, 8	24, 24	32, 14	4, 4	8, 8	24, 24	32, 32
FT	S	4, 4, 4	8, 4, 4	24, 24, 24	32, 32, 32	4, 4, 4	8, 4, 4	24, 24, 12	32, 32, 16	4, 4, 4	8, 4, 4	24, 24, 12	32, 32, 32
		4, 4	4, 5	24, 8	32, 14	4, 2	4, 2	12, 6	16, 6	4, 3	4, 2	24, 8	30, 8
	M	4, 4, 4	8, 7, 4	24, 24, 24	32, 32, 32	4, 4, 4	8, 4, 4	24, 24, 22	32, 32, 32	4, 4, 4	8, 7, 4	24, 24, 24	32, 32, 32
		4, 4	8, 5	24, 12	32, 32	4, 2	4, 2	22, 6	32, 6	4, 3	4, 2	22, 12	32, 8

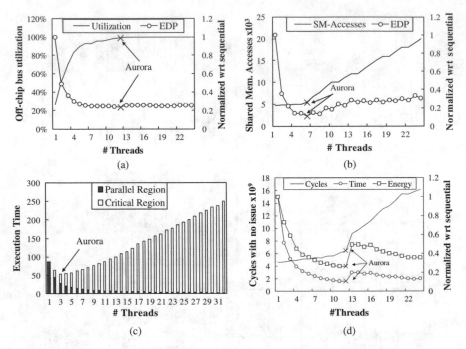

Fig. 5.5 Scalability behavior. (**a**) HPCG—2nd parallel region. (**b**) SP—1st parallel region. (**c**) *n*-body. (**d**) Hotspot

executing on the 24-core system. In this case, the optimal number of threads for EDP is 12 (see Table 5.4). As Fig. 5.5d shows, when increasing the number of threads from 12 to 13, the number of cycles that the threads spend without issuing any instruction abruptly increases. Therefore, performance decreases and energy consumption increases (Fig. 5.5d). Once more, by avoiding the excessive increment in the number of threads, Aurora improved performance by 21% and reduced EDP and energy by 44% and 25%, respectively.

Finally, as discussed in Chap. 1, it is important to note that there are cases in which the characteristic that influences the thread scalability changes according to the input set (Table 5.2). As a specific example, let us consider JA application. When it is executed with the small input set, the time that the threads spend synchronizing limits the application scalability. When executed with the medium input set, the off-chip bus becomes the main limiting factor because of the larger amount of data available.

5.3.2.2   Performance, Energy, and EDP

Table 5.4 depicts the number of threads found by Aurora that offers the best result in performance, energy, and EDP to execute the main parallel regions of each application. As an example, let us consider the LU application executing with the medium input on the 8-core system and targeting the EDP. It has two main parallel regions: the ideal number of threads for the first is four, while for the second the number is three. Moreover, depending on the input set, the ideal number of threads for each parallel region may vary. This is the case of the CG application running on the 32-core system. When changing the input set from small to medium, the workload of the second parallel region changes, increasing its TLP. Now, the best EDP for this region is achieved with 32 threads instead of 16. The ideal number of threads also varies when the target optimization metric changes. The ST executing on the 32-core system is an example: 12 threads is the best choice for performance, 4 threads for energy consumption, and 6 threads for EDP.

Figures 5.6, 5.7, and 5.8 present the results for the entire benchmark set when running the medium input set, along with their geometric mean (Gmean)

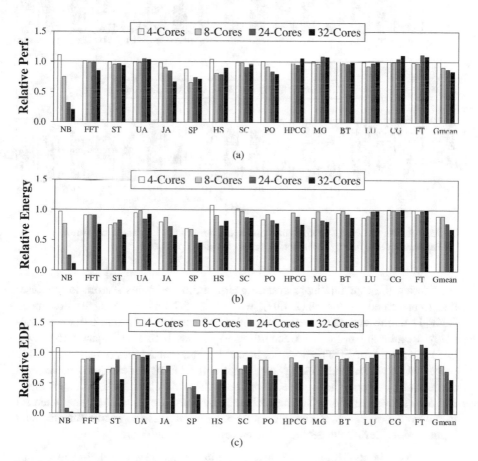

Fig. 5.6 Aurora vs Baseline (medium input): lower than 1.0 means that Aurora is better. (**a**) Performance. (**b**) Energy consumption. (**c**) Energy-delay product

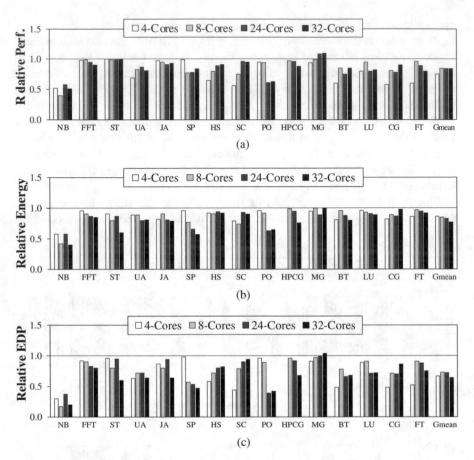

Fig. 5.7 Aurora vs OMP_Dynamic (medium input): lower than 1.0 means that Aurora is better.
(**a**) Performance. (**b**) Energy consumption. (**c**) Energy-delay product

considering the four multicore systems. Figure 5.6 compares Aurora to the baseline (represented by the black line), while Figs. 5.7 and 5.8 compare Aurora to OMP_Dynamic and FDT framework (also represented by a black line), respectively. Results are normalized according to the setup to be compared (baseline, OMP_Dynamic, or FDT), so values below 1 mean that Aurora is better. They are presented for performance, energy consumption, and EDP. For each metric, we show the result for Aurora when it is set to optimize the particular metric. As an example, Fig. 5.6b shows the energy savings achieved by Aurora over the baseline when set to reduce the energy consumption. Table 5.4 summarizes the results for the small input set considering the geometric mean for the four multicore systems.

Aurora Versus Baseline As observed in Fig. 5.6 and Table 5.4, in most cases Aurora shows improvements regarding any metric. If one considers the geometric mean (Gmean bars in each figure) in any scenario, Aurora is most of the times

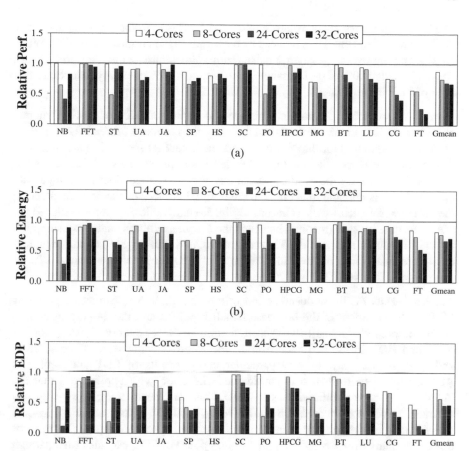

Fig. 5.8 Aurora vs FDT (medium input): lower than 1.0 means that Aurora is better. (**a**) Performance. (**b**) Energy consumption. (**c**) Energy-delay product

Table 5.4 Summary of the results for the small input w.r.t. the geometric mean: lower than 1.0 means that Aurora is better

	Performance			Energy			EDP		
	Baseline	OMP	FDT	Baseline	OMP	FDT	Baseline	OMP	FDT
4-core	0.98	0.75	0.84	0.91	0.85	0.83	0.90	0.63	0.72
8-core	0.91	0.83	0.78	0.89	0.85	0.80	0.80	0.71	0.62
24-core	0.85	0.81	0.67	0.76	0.83	0.67	0.68	0.70	0.44
32-core	0.88	0.84	0.69	0.66	0.78	0.73	0.54	0.62	0.48

better. In very specific scenarios where the design space exploration is limited, it presents similar results as the baseline. Considering the best case, execution time was reduced by 16% with the medium input set executing on the 32-core system.

The best scenario for energy consumption and EDP is with the small input set and the 32-core system: energy is reduced by 34%, and EDP is improved by 47%. When considering the overall geometric mean (entire benchmark set and all processors), Aurora provided 10% of performance improvements, 20% of energy reductions, and 28% of EDP improvements.

Aurora Versus OMP_Dynamic This specific implementation of OMP_Dynamic considers the last 15 min of execution to define the number of threads [22]. It does not use any search algorithm nor considers each parallel region in particular. For this reason, it is worse than the OpenMP baseline in many cases. The advantage of potentially decreasing the overhead, since it is not often called, does not compensate the fact that it is not able to get near to the optimal number of threads. Considering the best case for each metric (Gmean) in Fig. 5.6 and Table 5.4 Aurora reduced the execution time by 26% (medium input and the 4-core machine), energy consumption by 24% (medium input and the 32-core system), and EDP by 38% (small input and the 4-core system). In the overall (Gmean), Aurora was 11% faster, saved 17% of energy, and improved EDP by 32%.

Aurora Versus FDT As observed in Fig. 5.8 and Table 5.4, Aurora outperforms FDT in all scenarios. In the best case (small input set and the 24-core machine), Aurora improved (Gmean) the execution time by 34%, energy consumption by 34%, and EDP by 56%. In the overall, the improvements were of 26%, 25%, and 45%, respectively. In very particular cases, results of FDT are similar as Aurora's when performance is considered. These are with applications that are in the group of scalability issues that FDT handles, such as FFT (off-chip bus saturation) and JA (synchronization). However, as already discussed, FDT ignores many fundamental hardware characteristics, converging to a non-optimal number of threads in many times. Moreover, the training phase of FDT executes each parallel region in single-threaded mode until the standard deviation of the observed metric (memory bandwidth usage or synchronization time) is stable. It leads to a higher overhead for applications that present medium or high TLP. Because of this, in many cases FDT is worse than the baseline and OMP_Dynamic.

Varuna-PM One representative application was selected from each benchmark class (NB, SC, ST, and FT) and implemented them using the programming model employed by Varuna. They were executed with two different amounts of threads (1566 and 10k threads, taken from [113]) on the 32-core machine. Table 5.5 shows that these versions are slower than the OpenMP baseline. In particular, for the NB benchmark, which has its scalability limited by data-synchronization, the greater the number of threads, the greater the time the threads spend synchronizing. This increases the execution time and energy consumption (as discussed in Chap. 3). It is important to emphasize that these results do not consider the improvements provided by the analytic engine and the manager system of Varuna. However, even if the analytic engine could improve performance by 15% and reduce energy consumption by 31% (values taken from [113]), it would not be enough to provide the same levels of performance and energy as the OpenMP baseline, in most cases. The main

Table 5.5 Times that Varuna-PM is slower than baseline

# threads	Metric	Small				Medium			
		FT	SC	ST	NB	FT	SC	ST	NB
1566	Performance	1.8	1.6	1.3	164.4	1.8	2.0	1.2	161.7
	Energy	1.4	1.1	1.0	33.0	1.4	1.6	1.1	45.0
	EDP	2.5	1.8	1.4	5421.6	2.6	3.1	1.3	7274.8
10k	Performance	3.1	6.6	3.6	1020.8	2.1	3.7	2.2	1026.9
	Energy	1.9	4.5	2.4	204.8	1.6	2.7	1.5	1026.0
	EDP	5.9	29.6	8.6	209072	3.3	10.1	3.3	1053593

reason for these results is that Varuna was developed to be used in different kinds of applications (e.g., big data and ones that are recursively implemented), since it creates as many threads as possible. Therefore, Aurora and Varuna can be seen as two orthogonal approaches.

5.3.2.3 Distinct Approaches, Similar Convergence

Genetic algorithm is a search metaheuristic based on natural selection and genetics. It uses a concept of a population, which is a set of individual solutions (chromosomes), that can evolve to an optimum solution through generations. As GA requires minimum previous information on the problem at hand, it is widely used in many different situations. For our experiments, we started with a random population with a fixed size of 30 to 40 individuals (depending on the application). We modeled the chromosome to represent the global solution (i.e., the number of threads for each parallel region). Thus, we had to run the entire application for each new chromosome. Our population evolved by randomly selecting new chromosomes, giving higher chances for those with the best results in EDP. While applying the crossover guarantees the propagation of the best individuals characteristics, the mutation ensures the whole solution space can be searched. The probability for the crossover and the mutation to happen is of 0.9 and 0.001, respectively.

While the GA performs a global search, trying for different combinations for each parallel region, Aurora splits the problem into local searches (one for each region). The GA does find local optimums and escape them through the generations. However, it tends to perform worse when the space exploration is too large, represented by applications with many parallel regions. GMEAN_GA in Fig 5.9 shows the EDP (y-axis) given by the geometric mean of our benchmark set through the generations (x-axis). We also include the geometric mean of Aurora's execution (GMEAN_AURORA). All the results are normalized by the Oracle execution (represented as the constant line in 1). GMEAN_GA and GMEAN_AURORA lines clearly show that the GA converges to a similar result as Aurora over the generations (Fig. 5.9 truncates at generation 26), and when one considers the geometric mean, Aurora performs slightly better. We can also see the worst

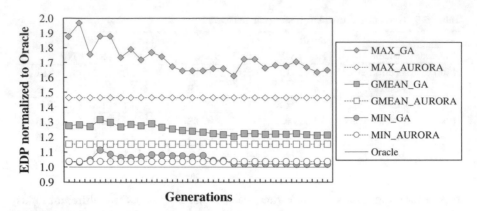

Fig. 5.9 Genetic algorithm convergence and Aurora

(MAX_GA and MAX_AURORA) and the best (MIN_GA and MIN_AURORA) cases from the executed applications for the GA and Aurora, respectively.

As observed, the GA can find better solutions than Aurora in its best case, but cannot achieve Aurora's result in the worst case (an application with many parallel regions) because of its coarse tuning characteristics. Furthermore, Fig. 5.9 omits the GA training time, which can easily exceed several hours and must be re-executed when anything in the system changes, such as the input size or microarchitecture. Aurora, on the other hand, can quickly adapt at runtime.

5.3.2.4   Evaluating the Efficiency of Aurora's Search Algorithm

Table 5.6 depicts (in percentage) how the results obtained by Aurora differ from the **Oracle** solution. We consider the geometric mean (Gmean) of the entire benchmark set for each processor and metric. The difference between ours and the optimal solution reflects the overhead of our technique, so we can measure the cost of the learning curve. As one can observe, these overheads are not very significant when compared to the best possible solution. The overhead is originated from two situations: the execution of the search algorithm itself, and the execution of a given parallel region with a number of threads that is not the ideal while the search algorithm is trying different possibilities to converge to the ideal number. Aurora showed higher overheads in the following situations:

1. The best result is achieved with either the maximum number of threads or a number close to it, which is the case of the FT and CG benchmarks executing on the 24 and 32-core systems.
2. The parallel region has a relatively small number of interactions but executes for a significant time, such as HPCG.

Table 5.6 Learning overheads (%) for Aurora w.r.t. the geometric mean for all the benchmarks

	Performance				Energy				EDP			
	4-core	8-core	24-core	32-core	4-core	8-core	24-core	32-core	4-core	8-core	24-core	32-core
S	0.7	0.9	2.9	9.9	0.9	1.4	0.9	4.1	1.8	2.1	2.6	6.6
M	1.0	0.7	2.4	3.1	0.9	2.0	1.6	3.0	2.8	1.9	2.5	5.4

3. Applications that have short execution time (i.e., less than 10 s), such as the MG. Its Oracle version takes only 1.45 s to execute on the 32-core system with the small input set.
4. Applications with many parallel regions, in which most of them have a low workload, as in the UA benchmark. UA has 54 parallel regions, and 44 of them take less than 0.5 s to execute regardless of the target processor.

Moreover, the higher the number of hardware threads available in the system, the greater the space exploration that must be covered. However, even though the overhead of the search algorithm increases, it does so in small rates, as can be observed when one compares the averages of the 24- and 32-core systems to the 4- and 8-core ones.

We also measured the execution time of the hill-climbing algorithm alone (considering only the specific calls to the respective function of the search algorithm). We consider the 32-core machine, which is the one that has the largest design space to be explored. Our experiments show that it presents an overhead of only 0.020% w.r.t. to the total execution time (geometric mean considering all benchmarks and inputs). In the worst case (MG benchmark, small input set), the search algorithm adds only 0.267% to the total execution time.

5.3.2.5   Limitations of Aurora

As already extensively discussed throughout this paper, Aurora works only with OpenMP and, more specifically, with the *OpenMP parallel directive*. However, it is important to remember that, as previously discussed in this chapter, *sections* and *tasks* are seldom used. In cases where there are parallel regions implemented in a different API or using unsupported OpenMP directives, Aurora will still work to find the ideal number of threads for each *OpenMP parallel directive* region. Therefore, it will not influence the execution of those other parallel regions.

Moreover, there are other scenarios where Aurora will also present some limitations: (1) The application is being parallelized to run on distributed systems, using some hybrid approach, in which the iterations of the outer loop are distributed to different nodes using a message passing library, and the inner loops are parallelized with OpenMP. For such hybrid approaches, Aurora will work for the OpenMP regions. (2) Multiple parallel loops are embedded inside an OpenMP parallel directive, using the clause *collapse*, which specifies how many loops in a nested loop should be collapsed into one large iteration space. In this scenario, Aurora will work to optimize the number of threads of the nested parallel loop. (3) The programmer wants to distribute the thread across the available sockets in an SMP architecture (e.g., match the number of threads of the outer loop with the number of sockets). Such applications will not benefit from Aurora's search algorithm because the number of threads for each parallel region is defined a priori (statically) by the programmer. This is usually done by very experienced programmers and is not significantly used nowadays.

Another requirement for Aurora is an interface to access performance counters for power dissipation and execution time. Current Intel platforms (all models manufactured after the Sandy Bridge microarchitecture, including i3, i5, i7, i9, Atom, Xeon, and Xeon Phi processors), AMD (some models from the Bobcat and Bulldozer family, and all models from the Zen family), and IBM Power9 Family provide all the hardware counters for execution time and power dissipation that Aurora needs. Some architectures (such as ARM) currently provide only the former, which prevent automatic optimization for energy and EDP. An alternative would be to estimate power based on the available performance counters, although this could lead to potentially wrong decisions by the search algorithm.

As observed in the experiments, Aurora presented its worst results executing applications with high TLP. In such cases, executing with the highest possible number of threads, as the baseline does, is already the best solution. Therefore, Aurora will waste time (1) with its learning algorithm and (2) executing the parallel regions with non-optimal number of threads during this process. In conclusion, when most parallel regions of an application have high TLP, Aurora may bring some small overhead compared to the baseline. Large input sets tend to alleviate this overhead, since each parallel region will proportionally execute more times using the ideal number of threads and less time in the process of learning.

Chapter 6
Conclusions

Efficiently exploiting thread-level parallelism has been challenging for software developers. As many parallel applications do not scale with the number of cores, not always using the maximum number of available cores running at the highest possible operating frequency will deliver the best performance or energy consumption. However, as discussed in this book, the task of rightly choosing the ideal amount of threads and the CPU operating frequency is not straightforward: many variables are involved (e.g., off-chip bus saturation and overhead of data-synchronization), which will change according to different aspects of the system at hand (e.g., input set, microarchitecture) and even during execution.

In this context, many works have been proposed to optimize the execution of parallel applications through the adaptation of the number of threads and the CPU operating frequency. As discussed in this book, they can be characterized according to the adaptability and transparency. The works that do not present adaptability at runtime can test many configurations without incurring in any overhead during the application execution, but their training time can take several hours. Besides that, when the environment changes, the offline analysis must be re-executed. On the other hand, approaches that provide adaptability at runtime can deal with the environment changes and select the ideal configuration as the application executes. However, this adaptability adds an overhead to the application execution. Therefore, runtime approaches must be efficient (find a solution close enough to the best possible one) and fast (converge to the solution within a few steps).

Most of the proposed approaches found in the literature and discussed in this book were designed to: (1) work only on homogeneous systems (same ISA and microarchitecture). Therefore, considering that heterogeneous multicore systems (HMS) are becoming more and more popular, we believe that one future direction is to design approaches to optimize the execution of applications in those systems.

A. Francisco Lorenzon, A. C. S. Beck Filho, *Parallel Computing Hits the Power Wall*, SpringerBriefs in Computer Science, https://doi.org/10.1007/978-3-030-28719-1_6

(2) target performance or energy. Nowadays, different non-functional requirements are becoming more important, such as the processor aging and reliability. (3) consider only one parallel API. However, heterogeneous systems may demand different communication models and, therefore, will probably need a mix of different APIs to communicate with each other.

References

1. Adya, A., Howell, J., Theimer, M., Bolosky, W.J., Douceur, J.R.: Cooperative task management without manual stack management. In: Annual Conference on USENIX, pp. 289–302. USENIX Association, Berkeley (2002)
2. Akram, S., Sartor, J.B., Eeckhout, L.: DVFS performance prediction for managed multi-threaded applications. In: ISPASS, pp. 12–23. IEEE, Piscataway (2016). https://doi.org/10.1109/ISPASS.2016.7482070
3. Alessi, F., Thoman, P., Georgakoudis, G., Fahringer, T., Nikolopoulos, D.S.: Application-level energy awareness for openmp. In: International Workshop on OpenMP, pp. 219–232. Springer, Berlin (2015)
4. Bailey, D.H., Barszcz, E., Barton, J.T., Browning, D.S., Carter, R.L., Dagum, L., Fatoohi, R.A., Frederickson, P.O., Lasinski, T.A., Schreiber, R.S., Simon, H.D., Venkatakrishnan, V., Weeratunga, S.K.: The NAS parallel benchmarks—summary and preliminary results. In: ACM/IEEE Conference on Supercomputing, pp. 158–165. ACM, New York (1991). https://doi.org/10.1145/125826.125925
5. Barnes, B.J., Rountree, B., Lowenthal, D.K., Reeves, J., de Supinski, B., Schulz, M.: A regression-based approach to scalability prediction. In: Proceedings of the 22Nd Annual International Conference on Supercomputing, ICS '08, pp. 368–377. ACM, New York (2008). https://doi.org/10.1145/1375527.1375580
6. Basmadjian, R., de Meer, H.: Evaluating and modeling power consumption of multi-core processors. In: 2012 Third International Conference on Future Systems: Where Energy, Computing and Communication Meet (e-Energy), pp. 1–10. IEEE, Piscataway (2012). https://doi.org/10.1145/2208828.2208840
7. Beck, A.C.S., Lisbôa, C.A.L., Carro, L.: Adaptable Embedded Systems. Springer, Berlin (2012)
8. Benedict, S., Rejitha, R.S., Gschwandtner, P., Prodan, R., Fahringer, T.: Energy prediction of openmp applications using random forest modeling approach. In: 2015 IEEE International Parallel and Distributed Processing Symposium Workshop, pp. 1251–1260. IEEE, Piscataway (2015). https://doi.org/10.1109/IPDPSW.2015.12
9. Benesty, J., Chen, J., Huang, Y., Cohen, I.: Pearson Correlation Coefficient, pp. 1–4. Springer, Berlin, (2009). https://doi.org/10.1007/978-3-642-00296-0_5
10. Bhatt, S., Chen, M., Lin, C.Y., Liu, P.: Abstractions for parallel *n*-body simulations. In: Scalable High Performance Computing Conference, pp. 38–45. IEEE, Piscataway (1992). https://doi.org/10.1109/SHPCC.1992.232690

11. Bhattacharjee, A., Martonosi, M.: Thread criticality predictors for dynamic performance, power, and resource management in chip multiprocessors. SIGARCH Comput. Archit. News **37**(3), 290–301 (2009). https://doi.org/10.1145/1555815.1555792

12. Blake, G., Dreslinski, R.G., Mudge, T., Flautner, K.: Evolution of thread-level parallelism in desktop applications. SIGARCH Comput. Archit. News **38**(3), 302–313 (2010)

13. Blem, E., Menon, J., Sankaralingam, K.: Power struggles: revisiting the RISC vs. CISC debate on contemporary arm and ×86 architectures. In: 2013 IEEE 19th International Symposium on High Performance Computer Architecture (HPCA), pp. 1–12. IEEE, Piscataway (2013). https://doi.org/10.1109/HPCA.2013.6522302

14. Browne, S., Dongarra, J., Garner, N., Ho, G., Mucci, P.: A portable programming interface for performance evaluation on modern processors. Int. J. High Perform. Comput. Appl. **14**(3), 189–204 (2000). https://doi.org/10.1177/109434200001400303

15. Browne, S., Dongarra, J., Garner, N., Ho, G., Mucci, P.: A portable programming interface for performance evaluation on modern processors. Int. J. High Perform. Comput. Appl. **14**(3), 189–204 (2000). https://doi.org/10.1177/109434200001400303

16. Buono, D., Matteis, T.D., Mencagli, G., Vanneschi, M.: Optimizing message-passing on multicore architectures using hardware multi-threading. In: 2014 22nd Euromicro International Conference on Parallel, Distributed, and Network-Based Processing, pp. 262–270. ACM, New York (2014). https://doi.org/10.1109/PDP.2014.63

17. Butenhof, D.R.: Programming with POSIX Threads. Addison-Wesley Longman Publishing, Boston (1997)

18. Cabrera, A., Almeida, F., Blanco, V., Giménez, D.: Analytical modeling of the energy consumption for the high performance linpack. In: 2013 21st Euromicro International Conference on Parallel, Distributed, and Network-Based Processing, pp. 343–350. IEEE, Piscataway (2013). https://doi.org/10.1109/PDP.2013.56

19. Cera, M., Pezzi, G., Mathias, E., Maillard, N., Navaux, P.: Improving the dynamic creation of processes in MPI-2. In: Recent Advances in Parallel Virtual Machine and Message Passing Interface pp. 247–255. Springer, Berlin (2006)

20. Chadha, G., Mahlke, S., Narayanasamy, S.: When less is more (limo): controlled parallelism forimproved efficiency. In: Proceedings of the 2012 International Conference on Compilers, Architectures and Synthesis for Embedded Systems, pp. 141–150. ACM, New York (2012)

21. Chandramowlishwaran, A., Knobe, K., Vuduc, R.: Performance evaluation of concurrent collections on high-performance multicore computing systems. In: 2010 IEEE International Symposium on Parallel Distributed Processing (IPDPS), pp. 1–12. IEEE, Piscataway (2010). https://doi.org/10.1109/IPDPS.2010.5470404

22. Chapman, B., Jost, G., Pas, R.v.d.: Using OpenMP: Portable Shared Memory Parallel Programming (Scientific and Engineering Computation). MIT Press, Cambridge, MA (2007)

23. Che, S., Boyer, M., Meng, J., Tarjan, D., Sheaffer, J.W., Lee, S.H., Skadron, K.: Rodinia: a benchmark suite for heterogeneous computing. In: IEEE International Symposium on Workload Characterization, pp. 44–54. IEEE Computer Society, Washington (2009). https://doi.org/10.1109/IISWC.2009.5306797

24. Chen, Y.L., Chang, M.F., Liang, W.Y., Lee, C.H.: Performance and energy efficient dynamic voltage and frequency scaling scheme for multicore embedded system. In: IEEE ICCE, pp. 58–59. IEEE, Piscataway (2016). https://doi.org/10.1109/ICCE.2016.7430521

25. Chou, C.Y., Chang, H.Y., Wang, S.T., Huang, K.C., Shen, C.Y.: An improved model for predicting hpl performance. In: Cérin, C., Li, K.C. (eds.) Advances in Grid and Pervasive Computing, pp. 158–168. Springer, Berlin (2007)

26. Christmann, C., Hebisch, E., Weisbecker, A.: Oversubscription of computational resources on multicore desktop systems. In: International Conference on Multicore Software Engineering, Performance, and Tools, MSEPT'12, pp. 18–29. Springer, Berlin (2012)

27. Cochran, R., Hankendi, C., Coskun, A.K., Reda, S.: Pack & cap: adaptive DVFS and thread packing under power caps. In: IEEE/ACM MICRO, pp. 175–185 (2011). https://doi.org/10.1145/2155620.2155641

28. Curtis-Maury, M., Dzierwa, J., Antonopoulos, C.D., Nikolopoulos, D.S.: Online power-performance adaptation of multithreaded programs using hardware event-based prediction. In: Proceedings of the 20th Annual International Conference on Supercomputing, pp. 157–166. ACM, New York (2006)

29. Curtis-Maury, M., Shah, A., Blagojevic, F., Nikolopoulos, D.S., De Supinski, B.R., Schulz, M.: Prediction models for multi-dimensional power-performance optimization on many cores. In: Proceedings of the 17th International Conference on Parallel Architectures and Compilation Techniques, pp. 250–259. ACM, New York (2008)

30. Dimakopoulos, V.V., Leontiadis, E., Tzoumas, G.: A portable c compiler for openmp v. 2.0. In: Proceedings of the of the 5th European Workshop on OpenMP (EWOMP03) (2003)

31. Ding, Y., Kandemir, M., Raghavan, P., Irwin, M.J.: A helper thread based edp reduction scheme for adapting application execution in CMPS. In: 2008 IEEE International Symposium on Parallel and Distributed Processing, pp. 1–14. IEEE, Piscataway (2008). https://doi.org/10.1109/IPDPS.2008.4536297

32. Dongarra, J., Heroux, M.A., Luszczek, P.: HPCG benchmark: a new metric for ranking high performance computing systems. Knoxville, Tennessee (2015)

33. dos Santos Marques, W., de Souza, P.S.S., Lorenzon, A.F., Beck, A.C.S., Beck Rutzig, M., Diniz Rossi, F.: Improving EDP in multi-core embedded systems through multidimensional frequency scaling. In: 2017 IEEE International Symposium on Circuits and Systems (ISCAS), pp. 1–4. IEEE, Piscataway (2017). https://doi.org/10.1109/ISCAS.2017.8050515

34. Dutot, P.F., Georgiou, Y., Glesser, D., Lefevre, L., Poquet, M., Rais, I.: Towards energy budget control in HPC. In: IEEE/ACM International Symposium on Cluster, Cloud and Grid Computing, pp. 381–390. IEEE, Piscataway (2017)

35. Esmaeilzadeh, H., Blem, E., St. Amant, R., Sankaralingam, K., Burger, D.: Power limitations and dark silicon challenge the future of multicore. ACM Trans. Comput. Syst. 30(3), 11:1–11:27 (2012). https://doi.org/10.1145/2324876.2324879

36. Foster, I.: Designing and Building Parallel Programs: Concepts and Tools for Parallel Software Engineering. Addison-Wesley Longman Publishing, Boston (1995)

37. Ge, R., Feng, X., Feng, W., Cameron, K.W.: CPU MISER: a performance-directed, run-time system for power-aware clusters. In: ICPP, pp. 18–18 (2007). https://doi.org/10.1109/ICPP.2007.29

38. Gropp, W., Lusk, E., Skjellum, A.: Using MPI (2Nd Ed.): Portable Parallel Programming with the Message-passing Interface. MIT Press, Cambridge (1999)

39. Hackenberg, D., Ilsche, T., Schone, R., Molka, D., Schmidt, M., Nagel, W.E.: Power measurement techniques on standard compute nodes: a quantitative comparison. In: IEEE International Symposium on Performance Analysis of Systems and Software, pp. 194–204. IEEE, Piscataway (2013). https://doi.org/10.1109/ISPASS.2013.6557170

40. Hähnel, M., Döbel, B., Völp, M., Härtig, H.: Measuring energy consumption for short code paths using RAPL. SIGMETRICS Perform. Eval. Rev. 40(3), 13–17 (2012). https://doi.org/10.1145/2425248.2425252

41. Ham, T.J., Chelepalli, B.K., Xue, N., Lee, B.C.: Disintegrated control for energy-efficient and heterogeneous memory systems. In: IEEE HPCA, pp. 424–435. IEEE, Piscataway (2013). https://doi.org/10.1109/HPCA.2013.6522338

42. Hankendi, C., Coskun, A.K.: Adaptive power and resource management techniques for multi-threaded workloads. In: 2013 IEEE International Symposium on Parallel Distributed Processing, Workshops and Phd Forum, pp. 2302–2305. IEEE, Piscataway (2013). https://doi.org/10.1109/IPDPSW.2013.258

43. Hennessy, J.L., Patterson, D.A.: Computer Architecture: A Quantitative Approach, 3rd edn. Morgan Kaufmann Publishers, San Francisco (2003)

44. Hoefler, T., Lumsdaine, A., Rehm, W.: Implementation and performance analysis of non-blocking collective operations for MPI. In: Proceedings of the 2007 ACM/IEEE Conference on Supercomputing, SC '07, pp. 52:1–52:10. ACM, New York (2007). https://doi.org/10.1145/1362622.1362692

45. Hotta, Y., Sato, M., Kimura, H., Matsuoka, S., Boku, T., Takahashi, D.: Profile-based optimization of power performance by using dynamic voltage scaling on a pc cluster. In: IEEE IPDPS (2006). https://doi.org/10.1109/IPDPS.2006.1639597

46. Hsu, C.H., Feng, W.C.: A power-aware run-time system for high-performance computing. In: Proceedings of the 2005 ACM/IEEE Conference on Supercomputing, SC '05, pp. 1–1 (2005). https://doi.org/10.1109/SC.2005.3

47. Hu, Z., Buyuktosunoglu, A., Srinivasan, V., Zyuban, V., Jacobson, H., Bose, P.: Microarchitectural techniques for power gating of execution units. In: Proceedings of the 2004 International Symposium on Low Power Electronics and Design, ISLPED '04, pp. 32–37. ACM, New York (2004). https://doi.org/10.1145/1013235.1013249

48. Hwang, Y., Chung, K.: Dynamic power management technique for multicore based embedded mobile devices. IEEE Trans. Ind. Inf. **9**(3), 1601–1612 (2013). https://doi.org/10.1109/TII.2012.2232299

49. Ipek, E., de Supinski, B.R., Schulz, M., McKee, S.A.: An approach to performance prediction for parallel applications. In: Proceedings of the 11th International Euro-Par Conference on Parallel Processing, Euro-Par'05, pp. 196–205. Springer, Berlin (2005)

50. Jayakumar, A., Murali, P., Vadhiyar, S.: Matching application signatures for performance predictions using a single execution. In: 2015 IEEE International Parallel and Distributed Processing Symposium, pp. 1161–1170. IEEE, Picataway (2015). https://doi.org/10.1109/IPDPS.2015.20

51. Joao, J.A., Suleman, M.A., Mutlu, O., Patt, Y.N.: Bottleneck identification and scheduling in multithreaded applications. In: International Conference on Architectural Support for Programming Languages and Operating Systems, pp. 223–234. ACM, New York (2012). https://doi.org/10.1145/2150976.2151001

52. Johnson, A., Jacobson, S.: On the convergence of generalized hill climbing algorithms. Discret. Appl. Math. **119**(1), 37–57 (2002). Special Issue devoted to Foundation of Heuristics in Combinatorial Optimization

53. Jordan, H., Thoman, P., Durillo, J.J., Pellegrini, S., Gschwandtner, P., Fahringer, T., Moritsch, H.: A multi-objective auto-tuning framework for parallel codes. In: International Conference for High Performance Computing, Networking, Storage and Analysis, pp. 1–12. IEEE, Picataway (2012)

54. Ju, T., Wu, W., Chen, H., Zhu, Z., Dong, X.: Thread count prediction model: Dynamically adjusting threads for heterogeneous many-core systems. In: 2015 IEEE 21st International Conference on Parallel and Distributed Systems (ICPADS), pp. 456–464. IEEE, Picataway (2015). https://doi.org/10.1109/ICPADS.2015.64

55. Jung, C., Lim, D., Lee, J., Han, S.: Adaptive execution techniques for SMT multiprocessor architectures. In: Proceedings of the Tenth ACM SIGPLAN Symposium on Principles and Practice of Parallel Programming, pp. 236–246. ACM, New York (2005)

56. Kahng, A.B., Kang, S., Rosing, T.S., Strong, R.: Many-core token-based adaptive power gating. IEEE Trans. Comput. Aided Des. Integr. Circuits Syst. **32**(8), 1288–1292 (2013). https://doi.org/10.1109/TCAD.2013.2257923

57. Karlin, I., Keasler, J., Neely, R.: Lulesh 2.0: updates and changes. pp. 1–9 (2013)

58. Kaxiras, S., Martonosi, M.: Computer Architecture Techniques for Power-Efficiency, 1st edn. Morgan and Claypool Publishers (2008)

59. Keating, M., Flynn, D., Aitken, R., Gibbons, A., Shi, K.: Low Power Methodology Manual: For System-on-Chip Design. Springer, Berlin (2007)

60. Kontorinis, V., Shayan, A., Tullsen, D.M., Kumar, R.: Reducing peak power with a table-driven adaptive processor core. In: Proceedings of the 42nd Annual IEEE/ACM International Symposium on Microarchitecture, MICRO 42, pp. 189–200. ACM, New York (2009). https://doi.org/10.1145/1669112.1669137

61. Korthikanti, V.A., Agha, G.: Towards optimizing energy costs of algorithms for shared memory architectures. In: Proceedings of the 22nd Annual ACM Symposium on Parallelism in Algorithms and Architectures (SPAA 2010) Thira, Santorini, Greece, June 13–15, 2010, pp. 157–165 (2010). https://doi.org/10.1145/1810479.1810510

62. Le Sueur, E., Heiser, G.: Dynamic voltage and frequency scaling: the laws of diminishing returns. In: Proceedings of the 2010 International Conference on Power Aware Computing and Systems, HotPower'10, pp. 1–8. USENIX Association, Berkeley (2010)
63. Lee, J., Wu, H., Ravichandran, M., Clark, N.: Thread tailor: dynamically weaving threads together for efficient, adaptive parallel applications. ACM SIGARCH Comput. Archit. News 38(3), 270–279 (2010)
64. Levy, H.M., Lo, J.L., Emer, J.S., Stamm, R.L., Eggers, S.J., Tullsen, D.M.: Exploiting choice: Instruction fetch and issue on an implementable simultaneous multithreading processor. In: International Symposium on Computer Architecture, pp. 191–191 (1996). https://doi.org/10.1145/232973.232993
65. Li, D., de Supinski, B.R., Schulz, M., Cameron, K., Nikolopoulos, D.S.: Hybrid MPI/openMP power-aware computing. In: IEEE IPDPS, pp. 1–12 (2010). https://doi.org/10.1109/IPDPS.2010.5470463
66. Li, D., de Supinski, B.R., Schulz, M., Nikolopoulos, D.S., Cameron, K.W.: Strategies for energy-efficient resource management of hybrid programming models. IEEE Trans. Parallel Distrib. Syst. 24(1), 44–157 (2013). https://doi.org/10.1109/TPDS.2012.95
67. Li, J., Martinez, J.F.: Dynamic power-performance adaptation of parallel computation on chip multiprocessors. In: The Twelfth International Symposium on High-Performance Computer Architecture, 2006, pp. 77–87 (2006). https://doi.org/10.1109/HPCA.2006.1598114
68. Lorenzon, A.F., Cera, M.C., Beck, A.C.S.: On the influence of static power consumption in multicore embedded systems. In: 2015 IEEE International Symposium on Circuits and Systems (ISCAS), pp. 1374–1377. IEEE, Piscataway (2015)
69. Lorenzon, A.F., Cera, M.C., Schneider Beck, A.C.: Performance and energy evaluation of different multi-threading interfaces in embedded and general purpose systems. J. Signal Process. Syst. 80(3), 295–307 (2015). https://doi.org/10.1007/s11265-014-0925-9
70. Lorenzon, A.F., Sartor, A.L., Cera, M.C., Beck, A.C.S.: Optimized use of parallel programming interfaces in multithreaded embedded architectures. In: 2015 IEEE Computer Society Annual Symposium on VLSI, pp. 410–415. IEEE, Piscataway (2015)
71. Lorenzon, A.F., Cera, M.C., Beck, A.C.S.: Investigating different general-purpose and embedded multicores to achieve optimal trade-offs between performance and energy. J. Parallel Distrib. Comput. 95(C), 107–123 (2016). https://doi.org/10.1016/j.jpdc.2016.04.003
72. Lorenzon, A.F., Souza, J.D., Beck, A.C.S.: Laant: A library to automatically optimize edp for openMP applications. In: DATE, pp. 1229–1232 (2017). https://doi.org/10.23919/DATE.2017.7927176
73. Lorenzon, A.F., de Oliveira, C.C., Souza, J.D., Beck, A.C.S.: Aurora: seamless optimization of openMP applications. IEEE Trans. Parallel Distrib. Syst. 30(5), 1007–1021 (2019). https://doi.org/10.1109/TPDS.2018.2872992
74. Luk, C.K., Cohn, R., Muth, R., Patil, H., Klauser, A., Lowney, G., Wallace, S., Reddi, V.J., Hazelwood, K.: Pin: Building customized program analysis tools with dynamic instrumentation. In: Proceedings of the 2005 ACM SIGPLAN Conference on Programming Language Design and Implementation, PLDI '05, pp. 190–200. ACM, New York (2005). https://doi.org/10.1145/1065010.1065034
75. Lungu, A., Bose, P., Buyuktosunoglu, A., Sorin, D.J.: Dynamic power gating with quality guarantees. In: Proceedings of the 2009 ACM/IEEE International Symposium on Low Power Electronics and Design, ISLPED '09, pp. 377–382. ACM, New York (2009). https://doi.org/10.1145/1594233.1594331
76. Madan, N., Buyuktosunoglu, A., Bose, P., Annavaram, M.: A case for guarded power gating for multi-core processors. In: 2011 IEEE 17th International Symposium on High Performance Computer Architecture, pp. 291–300 (2011). https://doi.org/10.1109/HPCA.2011.5749737
77. Marathe, A., Bailey, P.E., Lowenthal, D.K., Rountree, B., Schulz, M., de Supinski, B.R.: A run-time system for power-constrained hpc applications. In: Kunkel, J.M., Ludwig, T. (eds.) High Performance Computing, pp. 394–408. Springer, Cham (2015)

78. McCalpin, J.D.: Memory bandwidth and machine balance in current high performance computers. In: IEEE Computer Society Technical Committee on Computer Architecture Newsletter, pp. 19–25 (1995)
79. McCool, M., Reinders, J., Robison, A.: Structured Parallel Programming: Patterns for Efficient Computation, 1st edn. Morgan Kaufmann Publishers, San Francisco (2012)
80. McVoy, L., Staelin, C.: Lmbench: Portable tools for performance analysis. In: Proceedings of the 1996 Annual Conference on USENIX Annual Technical Conference, ATEC '96, pp. 23–23. USENIX Association, Berkeley (1996)
81. Miftakhutdinov, R., Ebrahimi, E., Patt, Y.N.: Predicting performance impact of dvfs for realistic memory systems. In: 2012 45th Annual IEEE/ACM International Symposium on Microarchitecture, pp. 155–165 (2012). https://doi.org/10.1109/MICRO.2012.23
82. Miftakhutdinov, R.R.: Performance prediction for dynamic voltage and frequency scaling. Ph.D. thesis, The University of Texas (2014)
83. Nose, K., Sakurai, T.: Optimization of vdd and vth for low-power and high speed applications. In: Proceedings of the 2000 Asia and South Pacific Design Automation Conference, ASP-DAC '00, pp. 469–474. ACM, New York (2000). https://doi.org/10.1145/368434.368755
84. Oboril, F., Tahoori, M.B.: Extratime: Modeling and analysis of wearout due to transistor aging at microarchitecture-level. In: IEEE/IFIP International Conference on Dependable Systems and Networks (DSN 2012), pp. 1–12 (2012). https://doi.org/10.1109/DSN.2012.6263957
85. Olukotun, K., Hammond, L.: The future of microprocessors. Queue 3(7), 26–29 (2005). https://doi.org/10.1145/1095408.1095418
86. OpenMP, A.: Openmp 4.0: specification (2013)
87. Palermo, G., Silvano, C., Zaccaria, V.: An efficient design space exploration methodology for on-chip multiprocessors subject to application-specific constraints. In: 2008 Symposium on Application Specific Processors, pp. 75–82 (2008). https://doi.org/10.1109/SASP.2008.4570789
88. Patterson, D.A., Hennessy, J.L.: Computer Organization and Design, 5th edn. The Hardware/Software Interface, 5th edn. Morgan Kaufmann Publishers, San Francisco (2013)
89. Petersen, W., Arbenz, P.: Introduction to parallel computing: a practical guide with examples in C. Oxford Texts in Applied and Engineering Mathematics. Oxford University Press, Oxford (2004)
90. Porterfield, A., Fowler, R., Neyer, M.: Maestro: Dynamic runtime power and concurrency adaptation. In: Proceedings Workshop Managed Many-Core System, pp. 1–8
91. Porterfield, A.K., Olivier, S.L., Bhalachandra, S., Prins, J.F.: Power measurement and concurrency throttling for energy reduction in openMP programs. In: Parallel and Distributed Processing Symposium Workshops & PhD Forum (IPDPSW), 2013 IEEE 27th International, pp. 884–891. IEEE, Piscataway (2013)
92. Pusukuri, K.K., Gupta, R., Bhuyan, L.N.: Thread reinforcer: Dynamically determining number of threads via os level monitoring. In: 2011 IEEE International Symposium on Workload Characterization (IISWC), pp. 116–125. IEEE, Piscataway (2011)
93. Quinlan, D., Liao, C.: The rose source-to-source compiler infrastructure. In: Cetus Users and Compiler Infrastructure Workshop, in conjunction with PACT 2011 (2011)
94. Quinn, M.: Parallel Programming in C with MPI and OpenMP. McGraw-Hill Higher Education (2004)
95. Raasch, S.E., Reinhardt, S.K.: The impact of resource partitioning on SMT processors. In: International Conference on Parallel Architectures and Compilation Techniques, pp. 15–25 (2003). https://doi.org/10.1109/PACT.2003.1237998
96. Raman, A., Zaks, A., Lee, J.W., August, D.I.: Parcae: A system for flexible parallel execution. In: ACM SIGPLAN Conference on Programming Language Design and Implementation, PLDI '12, pp. 133–144. ACM, New York (2012)
97. Rauber, T., Rünger, G.: Parallel Programming: For Multicore and Cluster Systems, 2nd edn. Springer, Berlin (2013)

98. Rizvandi, N.B., Taheri, J., Zomaya, A.Y., Lee, Y.C.: Linear combinations of DVFS-enabled processor frequencies to modify the energy-aware scheduling algorithms. In: CCGRID, pp. 388–397 (2010). https://doi.org/10.1109/CCGRID.2010.38

99. Rossi, F.D., Storch, M., de Oliveira, I., Rose, C.A.F.D.: Modeling power consumption for dvfs policies. In: 2015 IEEE International Symposium on Circuits and Systems (ISCAS), pp. 1879–1882. IEEE, Piscataway (2015). https://doi.org/10.1109/ISCAS.2015.7169024

100. Rountree, B., Lowenthal, D.K., Schulz, M., de Supinski, B.R.: Practical performance prediction under dynamic voltage frequency scaling. In: 2011 International Green Computing Conference and Workshops, pp. 1–8 (2011). https://doi.org/10.1109/IGCC.2011.6008553

101. Sensi, D.D.: Predicting performance and power consumption of parallel applications. In: 2016 24th Euromicro International Conference on Parallel, Distributed, and Network-Based Processing (PDP), pp. 200–207 (2016). https://doi.org/10.1109/PDP.2016.41

102. Sensi, D.D., Torquati, M., Danelutto, M.: A reconfiguration algorithm for power-aware parallel applications. TACO 13(4), 43:1–43:25 (2016). https://doi.org/10.1145/3004054

103. Seo, S., Jo, G., Lee, J.: Performance characterization of the nas parallel benchmarks in opencl. In: IEEE International Symposium on Workload Characterization, pp. 137–148 (2011). https://doi.org/10.1109/IISWC.2011.6114174

104. Shafik, R.A., Das, A., Yang, S., Merrett, G., Al-Hashimi, B.M.: Adaptive energy minimization of openMP parallel applications on many-core systems. In: Proceedings of the 6th Workshop on Parallel Programming and Run-Time Management Techniques for Many-core Architectures, pp. 19–24. ACM, New York (2015)

105. Shafik, R.A., Das, A.K., Yang, S., Merrett, G.V., Al-Hashimi, B.: Thermal-aware adaptive energy minimization of open MP parallel applications (2015)

106. Sharkawi, S., DeSota, D., Panda, R., Indukuru, R., Stevens, S., Taylor, V., Wu, X.: Performance projection of HPC applications using spec cfp2006 benchmarks. In: 2009 IEEE International Symposium on Parallel Distributed Processing, pp. 1–12. IEEE, Piscataway (2009). https://doi.org/10.1109/IPDPS.2009.5161057

107. Singh, K., İpek, E., McKee, S.A., de Supinski, B.R., Schulz, M., Caruana, R.: Predicting parallel application performance via machine learning approaches: Research articles. Concurr. Comput. Pract. Exper. 19(17), 2219–2235 (2007). https://doi.org/10.1002/cpe.v19:17

108. Snowdon, D.C., Petters, S.M., Heiser, G.: Accurate on-line prediction of processor and memoryenergy usage under voltage scaling. In: Proceedings of the 7th ACM &Amp; IEEE International Conference on Embedded Software, EMSOFT '07, pp. 84–93. ACM, New York (2007). https://doi.org/10.1145/1289927.1289945

109. Snowdon, D.C., Van Der Linden, G., Petters, S.M., Heiser, G.: Accurate run-time prediction of performance degradation under frequency scaling. In: Workshop on Operating Systems Platforms for Embedded Real-Time applications, p. 58 (2007)

110. Sodhi, S., Subhlok, J., Xu, Q.: Performance prediction with skeletons. Clust. Comput. 11(2), 151–165 (2008). https://doi.org/10.1007/s10586-007-0039-2

111. Song, S.L., Barker, K., Kerbyson, D.: Unified performance and power modeling of scientific workloads. In: Proceedings of the 1st International Workshop on Energy Efficient Supercomputing, E2SC '13, pp. 4:1–4:8. ACM, New York (2013). https://doi.org/10.1145/2536430.2536435

112. Sridharan, S., Gupta, G., Sohi, G.S.: Holistic run-time parallelism management for time and energy efficiency. In: Proceedings of the 27th international ACM conference on International conference on supercomputing, pp. 337–348. ACM, New York (2013)

113. Sridharan, S., Gupta, G., Sohi, G.S.: Adaptive, efficient, parallel execution of parallel programs. ACM SIGPLAN Notices 49(6), 169–180 (2014)

114. Subramanian, L., Seshadri, V., Kim, Y., Jaiyen, B., Mutlu, O.: Mise: Providing performance predictability and improving fairness in shared main memory systems. In: IEEE International Symposium on High Performance Computer Architecture, pp. 639–650 (2013)

115. Suleman, M.A., Qureshi, M.K., Patt, Y.N.: Feedback-driven threading: power-efficient and high-performance execution of multi-threaded workloads on CMPS. SIGARCH Comput. Archit. News 36(1), 277–286 (2008). https://doi.org/10.1145/1353534.1346317

116. Taborda, D., Zdravkovic, L.: Application of a hill-climbing technique to the formulation of a new cyclic nonlinear elastic constitutive model. Comput. Geotech. **43**, 80—91 (2012)
117. Tanenbaum, A.S.: Modern Operating Systems, 3rd edn. Prentice Hall, Upper Saddle River (2007)
118. Taylor, V., Xu, X., Geisler, J., Li, X., Lan, Z., Hereld, M., Judson, I.R., Stevens, R.: Prophesy: automating the modeling process. In: Proceedings Third Annual International Workshop on Active Middleware Services, pp. 3–11 (2001). https://doi.org/10.1109/AMS.2001.993715
119. Taylor, V., Wu, X., Geisler, J., Stevens, R.: Using kernel couplings to predict parallel application performance. In: Proceedings 11th IEEE International Symposium on High Performance Distributed Computing, pp. 125–134 (2002). https://doi.org/10.1109/HPDC.2002.1029910
120. Tiwari, A., Laurenzano, M.A., Carrington, L., Snavely, A.: Modeling power and energy usage of hpc kernels. In: 2012 IEEE 26th International Parallel and Distributed Processing Symposium Workshops PhD Forum, pp. 990–998 (2012). https://doi.org/10.1109/IPDPSW.2012.121
121. Vogelsang, T.: Understanding the energy consumption of dynamic random access memories. In: Proceedings of the 2010 43rd Annual IEEE/ACM International Symposium on Microarchitecture, MICRO '43, pp. 363–374. IEEE Computer Society, Washington (2010). https://doi.org/10.1109/MICRO.2010.42
122. Wall, D.W.: Limits of instruction-level parallelism. In: Proceedings of the Fourth International Conference on Architectural Support for Programming Languages and Operating Systems, ASPLOS IV, pp. 176–188. ACM, New York (1991). https://doi.org/10.1145/106972.106991
123. Wheeler, K.B., Murphy, R.C., Thain, D.: Qthreads: An api for programming with millions of lightweight threads. In: IEEE International Symposium on Parallel and Distributed Processing, pp. 1–8 (2008). https://doi.org/10.1109/IPDPS.2008.4536359
124. Willhalm, T., Dementiev, R., Fay, P.: Intel performance counter monitor—a better way to measure cpu utilization. Tech. rep., Intel (2017)
125. Witkowski, M., Oleksiak, A., Piontek, T., Węglarz, J.: Practical power consumption estimation for real life HPC applications. Futur. Gener. Comput. Syst. **29**(1), 208–217 (2013). https://doi.org/10.1016/j.future.2012.06.003
126. Wu, Q., Martonosi, M., Clark, D.W., Reddi, V.J., Connors, D., Wu, Y., Lee, J., Brooks, D.: Dynamic-compiler-driven control for microprocessor energy and performance. IEEE Micro **26**(1), 119–129 (2006). https://doi.org/10.1109/MM.2006.9
127. Yang, L.T., Ma, X., Mueller, F.: Cross-platform performance prediction of parallel applications using partial execution. In: Proceedings of the 2005 ACM/IEEE Conference on Supercomputing, SC '05, p. 40. IEEE Computer Society, Washington (2005). https://doi.org/10.1109/SC.2005.20
128. Zhang, W., Cheng, A.M.K., Subhlok, J.: Dwarfcode: A performance prediction tool for parallel applications. IEEE Trans. Comput. **65**(2), 495–507 (2016). https://doi.org/10.1109/TC.2015.2417526

Printed in the United States
By Bookmasters